The Case for Reincarnation

James Dillet Freeman

Unity Books
Unity Village, MO 64065

Second Printing 1986

Cover designed by Sue Jackson
Cover photograph by Keith McKinney

What am I? What are you?
What country do we journey from?
What country do we journey to?
Out of a mystery we come
Into this mystery where we
Go to another mystery.

CONTENTS

Introduction

This book grew. It began twenty years ago as a thirty-minute talk about reincarnation. During the next fifteen years I made the talk in a number of different places, and it grew slowly to last an hour and a half. Then A.R.E., the Association of Research and Enlightenment, asked me to give some lectures at one of their symposiums. It grew again. Then Unity School for Religious Studies asked me to make six lectures on the subject for their Continuing Education Program. It grew a great deal. Then Unity School said it would like to make a tape based on the lectures. As I worked at this, it grew even more. In fact, it grew too long to be made into a tape, even two or three tapes. I realized that if it were going to be used, it would have to be a book.

I realized this reluctantly. Had I set out with the realization that what I was preparing was going to be put down on paper instead of spoken into the air, I would have approached it in a different way. But I had thought of what I was doing in no other way than as lectures.

There is a difference between oral and written communication.

As I transcribed what I had, converting spoken words into a typed manuscript, I saw that I had some two hundred pages of material, written in a conversational style, with many contractions, with sentences that are not complete sentences, with the humorous remarks and little asides that are the mark of the speaker. Also, I had freely borrowed material from my other books, sometimes altered, sometimes word for word.

I started to rewrite the manuscript to make it conform to what I considered good literary style; but the more I worked on rewriting, the more I felt that I was not only wasting my time, I was also doing anyone who might read my book an injury rather than a favor.

So the book would be in a conversational style? Wouldn't that make it easier to read? So it would contain pieces I had already written? These said exactly what I wanted to say, and some of them were the best writing I have ever done; to rewrite them would be a herculean and probably impossible task.

So I quit trying to rewrite what I had written, and I hope as you read this book, you will experience it as I originally created it—that is, as lectures.

If you have heard me speak, you know what it sounded like as I delivered it. If you've never heard me, you may imagine what it sounded like from this book.

I hope that, as you read, you will become as fascinated by the subject as I did when I lectured about it. The longer I worked at it, the more I could see that whether or not my thinking was throwing more light on the exact nature of the next life, there was no doubt that it was bringing me a keener insight into the nature of this life and helping me to find its meaning.

The longer I studied and the more I thought, the more I could see that you can't understand the meaning of life without taking death into account, and you can't understand the meaning of death without thinking about what life is.

I came to see that the best way to look at life and death is to see them not as two separate subjects, but as one continuous experience, intertwined and indivisible, each containing the other, each forming out of the other and dissolving into the other.

We are making an immortal journey, and the road winds round and round and up and up. Our view depends on which side of the mountain we are looking from.

Life After Death

On October 12, 1926, a little girl was born to a couple who lived in Delhi, India. They named her Kumari Shanti Devi. The little girl was different. She played by herself a great deal, and often would chatter about her husband and children. When she was nine, she told her parents that she wasn't Shanti Devi, she was Lugdi Chaubey. She and her husband, Kedar Nath Chaubey, had lived in Muttra. Muttra was a town a hundred miles away. In 1925, the year before she was born as Shanti Devi, she had died in childbirth.

Naturally, all this upset her family. Her parents tried to make her realize it was just her imagination, but she kept insisting it was true. Finally, an uncle decided to find out if there was a Kedar Nath Chaubey in Muttra. He wrote to him.

It turned out that there was, and he had a cousin in Delhi, so he asked this cousin to visit Shanti's family. Shanti immediately recognized him. During this meeting, he was so impressed by her answers to his questions that he wrote to Kedar Nath. Kedar Nath was flabbergasted. Wouldn't you be? He came to Delhi, bringing his ten-year-old son, who had been born to Lugdi Chaubey on September 25, 1925. The moment Shanti saw Kedar Nath, she recognized him. The two of them discussed private matters that only his former wife could know.

The newspapers got hold of the story, and Shanti was subjected to a great deal of questioning. She asked to be taken to Muttra. She had never been there.

When Shanti got off the train, there was a large crowd on the railway platform. She recognized her former husband's brother among them. Later, she picked her father, mother, and brother out of another crowd. Without help of any kind she led the way to the house where Lugdi Chaubey had lived, on the way pointing out buildings that had not been there when she had lived in Muttra. She showed great familiarity with the house which she claimed had once been hers. She even pointed out the spot in the garden where a well had been that was no longer there. Finally, she led the way to a room where she said she had buried some money. She told them the exact amount. Kedar Nath said that that was true, his former wife had done so, but he had dug the money up after her death. Lugdi had died at the age of 23, on October 4, 1925.

The story of Shanti Devi is a famous story in the field of paranormal occurrences. It was investigated and attested to by extremely reliable witnesses. It has fascinated many persons. It is a thought-stimulating story, isn't it?

Through the years, I have read a number of stories like Shanti Devi's. Probably you have, too. You may or may not believe them according to your bent of mind. My own first reaction when I hear one of these stories is to wonder whether it really happened; I think this is a natural reaction. But there are so many of these stories that just as it is hard to believe them, so it is also hard to believe that at least some of them are not genuine memories of previous lives. Certainly there is no doubt as to the sincerity and deep feeling of many of those who describe these experiences.

I have not based this case for reincarnation on stories like Shanti Devi's. If you believe them, they prove beyond question that reincarnation occurs. But too many persons question their authenticity. So I have based the case on the reasonableness of reincarnation, at least if you hope to believe in a reasonable way that there is life after death and that the world has meaning and is the work of a God who is intelligence and love. I have been encouraged in my belief by the fact that saints and poets and philosophers, artists and musicians and inventors and scientists, and the founders of many of the world's religions, a vast number of those whom we have to count as the most intelligent and the most spiritual people who have ever lived, have also believed this to be true—that reincarnation is the most reasonable explanation of the nature of things. It offers not only the most reasonable explanation of what life after death may be like, but also of how it is possible for the world we find ourselves in here and now to be what it is like.

Before I go on, let me tell you what I mean

4

when I say reincarnation. By reincarnation I mean that you have lived other lives before you began this one, lives that led you into your present existence. After you die, you will be reborn again, perhaps in this world, perhaps in others, perhaps in human form, perhaps in some much different mode of manifestation, but one that you will be drawn to by virtue of what you have become; and you will be reborn again and again until you have grown to be the perfect individual God meant you to grow to be when He made you.

Everyone has always been interested in death and dying and what life after death may be like. The existentialists say that our principal fear is that we all know we're going to die. The thought of dying lurks at the center of our being. I think that may be an exaggeration, but we are all interested—we all wonder.

A century or two ago, the idea of reincarnation would have been rejected by most Americans and Europeans as preposterous. A century ago, you would have believed that you were a soul made especially by God to be born into your present body to live this life; and after you died you would be judged by Him and sent on to heaven, a beautiful city in the sky, or to hell, a fiery pit under the earth—or if you were a Catholic, to purgatory.

But for the last hundred years there has been a rapidly growing number of people who cannot accept the old religious concepts. They want to believe in God and to believe that life has meaning, but the flood of scientific discoveries and insights has forced them to reconsider their ideas about the basic nature of the world we live in, its origins, its truths. They have found themselves having to question the teachings of the traditional churches on many points.

Sigmund Freud said: *The voice of the intelligence is weak, but it is persistent.* We are driven by habit, by emotional needs, and by social pressures to continue in established patterns of religious belief and behavior, but sooner or later our minds will force us to abandon beliefs that our reason finds unacceptable.

Some people are afraid to consider new ideas. Some people are so tightly bound to a creed that they dare not consider new ideas.

But today the traditional churches themselves are beginning to loosen their rigidities. Priests and preachers and rabbis are daring to believe they're not bound by beliefs their reason cannot accept. They are daring to look at their beliefs and incorporate new ideas in the way they present them.

Not that reincarnation is a new idea! It is one of the earliest, oldest, and most universal ideas we human beings have had. It was debated among the early Christians for hundreds of years and was believed in by at least as many as did not believe it, probably by more. Only after an authoritative church appeared that was powerful enough to suppress all beliefs except its own favorite ones, reincarnation was rejected as an un-Christian belief.

I suppose reincarnation can be presented in dogmatic ways that make it unacceptable to many devout Christians, just as Christianity has been presented in dogmatic ways that have made it unacceptable to many thoughtful people in our time. But I don't believe in reincarnation in a dogmatic way. I look at reincarnation as not only completely compatible with the important teachings of Christianity, but I think it makes Christianity more Christian.

I assume, since you are listening to these lectures, that you know I am associated with a comparatively new approach to religion called Unity, which began about a hundred years ago with the publication in 1889 of a small magazine called *Modern Thought.* Unity is one of a number of new religions which are usually referred to as metaphysical or New Thought religions. Unity is an American religion; I sometimes say it is Americanism in religion. It is a positive approach toward God and life. It teaches that God means your life to be good, but the quality of your life is up to you; life is consciousness.

Unity is an undogmatic approach to religion. That is the only kind of religion I could have. It offers its teachings, and it tells you to accept those that help you to live and live effectively. It says it is practical Christianity. In regard to reincarnation, Unity offers it as a reasonable suggestion; you can accept it or reject it as you feel led. Finally, after long thought, I decided that it is the most reasonable belief I could find. In fact, I came to wonder how anyone can have any other belief—if he wants to believe in a meaningful world and a just God.

I believe I've succeeded in these lectures in bringing together some ideas about reincarnation that any thoughtful person—believer or unbeliever—may find interesting, reasonable, and provocative. So I present these ideas for you to consider—not as dogma, but in the hope they'll not only help you to find some useful insights as to what the next life may be like, but also some insights that will help you to live this life more effectively, which is what all teaching should do, isn't it?

I'm not an authority on the subject of the next life, and I'm not anxious to become one, because as far as I know, there's only one way to do this. It's like the preacher who was making an impassioned sermon about heaven and how his religion would get you there. He said, "I've found the bus that takes you to heaven. How many of you want to get on the bus with me?" Everybody stood up except one little fellow in the front row. The peacher looked at him and said, "Don't you want to go to heaven?" He said, "Sure I do, preacher. I'd just like to take a later bus."

I'm not sure there are any real authorities on this subject of *the undiscover'd country from whose bourn no traveler returns.*

Many have described this country. For thousands of years we've had all kinds of descriptions, starting back in antiquity and running through Dante to various moderns who've written books about it. But one of the things that impresses me about these celestial and infernal travelogues is the great variance and disagreement among them. It has to make one wonder.

When I began this study I thought I had no interest in the subject. I've always told people I was like Emerson who said: *What I have seen teaches me to trust my Creator in what I have not seen.* And I've always told myself, "That's my feeling about it. My next life is something I don't have to worry about."

Maybe that's one of the reasons I like Unity. Unity is a this-world religion. Very strongly so. This-world! Charles Fillmore, a co-founder of Unity, said, "You learn nothing by dying. You learn by living and learning how to keep on being alive." That's why he rejected spiritualism. He tried it as a young man. He said, "The dead didn't know how to do what I want to do. They're over there dead. I want to learn how to live."

Jesus said something much in the same vein. He said: *"Do not be anxious about tomorrow, for tomorrow will be anxious for itself. Let the day's own trouble be sufficient for the day."* (Matt. 6:34) Well, it is, isn't it? Certainly for most of us.

I have known a few people who, when they

get to thinking about reincarnation, get so carried away with trying to find out what some of their past lives were that they have more interest in that than they do in solving the problems of this life. I don't want to do that, and I don't want you to do that. I don't see how it can be of value.

I'm not trying to find out what my past lives were, or worrying about what my next life will be. That's not why I'm interested in reincarnation. I'm interested in reincarnation because I hope that study of it will throw light on what this life is all about, and what it should be about.

What is this life all about? Does it make sense? If so, how? The beliefs I had as a child about the next life, beliefs I got from churches, my parents, and other children, have long seemed preposterous. What then can I believe? What is reincarnation? Is it possible and plausible? How can it take place? Why have so many people believed in it? Why have some people not believed in it?

I'm a seeker, an asker, a knocker at the door. I've never been able to believe something just because some authority pronounces it as true. I have to find out for myself, or at least try to find out. All my life I've gone to God and asked Him many questions, and most of the time He's answered me with many questions of His own, as He answered Job.

I am lecturing about reincarnation because I'm fascinated by the mystery of life, and a great part of this mystery consists in the mystery out of which it comes and the mystery into which it goes. This whole strange recurrent affair of life and death fascinates me. Doesn't it fascinate you?

Like the existentialists, I don't believe there's anybody who isn't fascinated by the thought of what happens when we die. I guess I've been fascinated by it all my life without realizing how fascinated I was.

Maybe that's the way it is with all of us. We don't want to bring it into our conscious thinking—most of us would like to obliterate the thought—but as the existentialists say, the subject lurks like a shadow in the back of our minds. We think about it, whether we want to or not. I believe what I have to say in these lectures will help you to think about it, in a positive way, in a helpful way, in an intelligent—a reasonable—way. When I began consciously to look into what I thought, I discovered I'd been writing about death and dying and the next life ever since I started writing. All kinds of pieces. I've written articles, I've written stories, I've written poems.

In fact, the very first poem I can remember writing was mainly about death and dying. I was ten years old, and my life had just gone through some hectic and frightening changes, and I began to write verse. Fortunately for you and me, I have lost the poems I wrote, but the first of them I called "The Storm." I can remember only four lines of it:

A man came by upon a plank,

But never would he reach the bank,

and it ended with the not very poetic couplet:

And barns and houses and trees all fall,

And in time to come so will we all.

A poem I wrote forty years ago is called "The Traveler." Maybe you have read it. Before I started to work out my ideas for these lectures, I called Unity School's shipping department and said, "How many 'Travelers' have you sent out to people?" They called me back a couple of days later and said, "We have sent out 983,000 'Travelers.'" That was more than four years ago, so it must be many more than a million by now. It's been reprinted by all kinds of people besides Unity—greeting card companies, magazines, even put into anthologies. As "The Traveler," I guess I've taken part in millions of funerals. Oh, I'm glad to have been there, because if there is ever a time when you need help, it's when you lose somebody dear to you. No question about that. That's one of the reasons we have such a need to know what happens. It's the main reason I'm making these talks.

I wrote "The Traveler" a long time ago, and I wrote it simply as a *Daily Word* lesson when I first started to write for *Daily Word* forty years ago. But the editors didn't think they should use it as a lesson. Instead they put it in the center of the magazine, and since then a lot of people have come up to me wherever I go and said, "You'll never know what your little poem has meant to me." Why don't I read it? Perhaps it states as simply and clearly as anything what I believe about the next life:

The Traveler

He has put on invisibility.
Dear Lord, I cannot see
But this I know, although the road
            ascends

And passes from my sight,
That there will be no night;
That You will take him gently by the
        hand
And lead him on
Along the road of life that never ends,
And he will find it is not death but
        dawn.
I do not doubt that You are there as
        here,
And You will hold him dear.

Our life did not begin with birth,
It is not of the earth;
And this that we call death, it is no
        more
Than the opening and closing of a
        door—
And in Your house how many rooms
        must be
Beyond this one where we rest
        momently.

Dear Lord, I thank You for the faith
        that frees,
The love that knows it cannot lose its
        own;

The love that, looking through the
    shadows, sees
That You and he and I are ever one!

Well, as I say, I'm not exactly sure as to
what the details of the next life will be, but
one thing I am sure of—yes, this is one thing
I am certain of—all my reason demands it:
there is no traditional heaven or hell as
they're generally thought of.

It's not that I don't believe we can and do
create a hellish state within us—most of us do
that too often—and even once in a while a
heavenly one. Milton was certainly right:

The mind is its own place, and in itself
Can make a heaven of hell, a hell of heaven.

It's just that I don't believe there are a
heaven and hell such as the traditional
churches have imagined—dwelling places in
the next world, to which we are transported
when we die, there to remain through everlasting—in a fiery pit if we were bad, in an
angelic city if we were good.

As to hell, I don't think there is any God
monstrous enough to make a hell. I cannot
believe in a God that mean. As somebody has
said, "With a God like this, who needs a
devil?"

Dante, from whom the medieval Christians

got most of their notions about the place, said that the sign above the gate read, "Abandon hope, all ye who enter here." It should have read, "Abandon reason, all you who believe in such a place."

As to heaven, I've never met a human being blissful enough—heaven is a state of perfect bliss, isn't it? I've never met anyone who, if he got into heaven, wouldn't shortly make it into something very different from heaven. I know if I got there, it would not be heavenly for long. And I don't think most people are much better than I am.

Whatever else you may imagine heaven to be, surely you cannot conceive it to be anything less than a place of perfect love. Ask yourself, how perfect is your love? Most of us human beings are not very loving. In fact, we're selfishly indifferent to one another's welfare. I feel this is the most important thing we human beings have to learn—to love one another. No, I've never met a human being good enough or loving enough that he'd keep it heavenly very long.

It's interesting. I've written a lot of pieces about a lot of subjects. Occasionally, in one of Unity's magazines, *Daily Word* or *Unity*, I've written that I don't believe in a traditional heaven and hell. When I do, a few people always write in and cancel their subscriptions. I am sorry to say this, but I do not believe it's my not believing in heaven that bothers them as much as my saying, "There ain't no hell," that makes them hellishly angry. It's like the story about the two different churches on opposite corners. One put up a sign, "There ain't no hell," so the other put up a sign, "The hell there ain't." Apparently people really want their hell. And they've occasionally written me and told me, "You'll find out, buddy!" They want to get me there! Like the evangelist who was having a revival meeting, giving his people fire and brimstone. Finally, he said, "There will be weeping and wailing and gnashing of teeth!" One little old lady stood up in the back row and said, "Preacher, I ain't got no teeth!" And he said, "Madam, teeth will be provided!" You're not going to get out because you don't have teeth.

Christianity is the religion of love. I've often wondered why so many traditional Christians want to make God so mean. I really wonder! Almost all religions believe in some form of heaven and hell, whether they also believe in reincarnation or not. But most of the others don't make hell eternal. Heaven and hell are just temporary stopping places, like this one. Christians make hell eternal. I don't understand it!

The Catholics do better. They have purgatory, unpleasant enough but not quite hell, and not for forever. I like the idea of purgatory, but as I've told people, where do you think you are now? If this life isn't purgatory, what is it?

In one of the bleak moments of my life I wrote a little four-line piece of verse:

When I consider what thoughts run
In my mind's madhouse cell,
I wonder if the earth is one
Of the suburbs of hell.

I am afraid many people reject reincarnation because they don't think it provides for enough punishment. Most people want to see anyone they think is a wrongdoer paying the penalty for his acts. They want him to be judged in his next life; they want him to suffer.

But how much we are suffering! We are judged daily. And the judgment—the reward for our good deeds and the punishment for our bad ones—is that we have to be what we have become. We don't go to hell because we commit evil deeds; we commit evil deeds because we are in hell—and we think that by violence or deceit we can break our way out. We writhe in searing flames of hate and fear, bound in the constricting bonds of selfness. If you imagine fire and brimstone to be worse, it is only because you are not aware of what is going on in the human soul, perhaps not even in your own.

It's not that I don't believe in heaven and hell. It's just that I don't believe in them as future eternal dwelling places.

Once I had a vision of hell. It was a genuine vision, at least as far as I am capable of knowing what a genuine vision is. I woke, and as I lay in my bed, suddenly I found myself being dragged down into hell. I got up and wrote my vision down. I put it in the first book I wrote for Doubleday, *Happiness Can Be A Habit*, one of the most mistitled books ever written. The publishers gave it that title, which has nothing to do with the contents, because they thought it would sell the book. It is now out of print.

The title makes the book sound like one on self-improvement by positive thinking. It was as unlike that as you can write a book. It was a poetic book about God. When people asked me what the book was about, I told them, "It's a poor man's 'Paradise Lost.'" I wrote my book for the same reason Milton said he wrote his epic poem, to "justify the ways of God to men."

Sometimes I feel that, like Spinoza, I am "a God-intoxicated man." I have a passion to believe in God. But like many persons in our time, I have found myself having to ask the question, "How is it possible to believe that this world is the work of a good God?" I have asked it over and over all my life. *I believe; help my unbelief!*" (Mark 9:24)

I have an intuitive sense of God's reality, even the mystic's sense of His presence, perhaps deeper and more intense than any other feeling in my life. But if I am God-tormented, I am also doubt-tormented—or do the doubts come from God? For I cannot settle for little gods.

My heart cries out, "O my God, how great You are!" You are love beyond my loveliest dream of love! You are intelligence beyond my highest understanding of intelligence! You are goodness beyond my power to measure good and evil! O my God, You are infinitely more than all I can conceive, or imagine, or experience You to be!

21

But God, You gave me a mind to think, and so I look at the world and ask, How can a world with so much cruelty in it, much of it man-made but much of it with natural causes, be the work of that which, if it has meaning at all, must be above all else intelligence and love?

I have written a great deal about this, and I think I've had some inspired, if not conclusive, ideas about it. But one provocative, debatable subject is enough at one time, for both the lecturer and his listeners, so in these lectures I am going to stick to reincarnation.

However, I've always felt a deep kinship with the little Jewish tailor who didn't go to the synagogue on Yom Kippur. His friends came the next day and said to him, "How could you have failed to go to the synagogue on Yom Kippur to repent your sins?"

"Oh," he said, "God and I have an understanding. I have told Him that if He will forgive my sins, I will forgive His."

You may ask how I can talk about being a believer when I have so many doubts.

I can only repeat after Tennyson,

There lives more faith in honest doubt,
Believe me, than in half the creeds.

Many years ago someone dear to me had a

mongoloid child, and I wrote a series of poems trying to answer the question, "How can Love let this happen?" I never finished them. Among them was one I called "Strength." I can never be sure what a poem will say to someone, but a number of people have told me that this one has said much to them, and I include it here in the hope that it may give you some idea of how faith and doubt can be so mixed together that you cannot be sure whether it is one or the other that is pressing you on.

Strength

Who was not threatened, never quailed;
Who was not tempted, never fell;
Who was not tested, never failed.
Go ask not of the quick and well,
But of the ones who agonize,
What wholeness is; the fallen only
Can tell you what it means to rise;
To learn of friendship ask the lonely.
Go ask the ones who broke and ran
What courage is, not those who stood;
None may know less of virtue than
The saint who has been only good.
For those who went beyond their
      strength

Alone can tell the measure of
The heart's capacities, the length
To which despair may go, or love.

Ever since I was a little boy, I have sensed how much pain there is in the world. I remember one night riding home in a streetcar, and there was no one else in the car except a black child about my size. There was a motorman, of course, but he was just part of the street-car, which says a great deal about how we often think of one another. As I rode in the brightly lighted streetcar through the dark city so crowded with so many people, each one trudging down his own special street I hardly knew the name of and probably would never walk along, each one dwelling behind his own curtained windows of rooms I would never see, each one a stranger to all but a handful, each one going his own personal way, caught in his own web of habit and hap-penstance—all so unknown to me but all so like me, suddenly a sense of identity with all other human beings poured overwhelmingly over me. I stared at the other boy, so like me, yet so unlike me, and suddenly I was the little black child in the big white world. Perhaps it was only my own pain and my own feelings of rage and rejection that I found myself projecting as his, but I found myself praying, "Lord, help me to help people not to hurt so much!" I have prayed that prayer all my life: "O God, help me to help people not to hurt so much. Help me to help people to live."

That is why I have spent my life serving in Silent Unity, a ministry of prayer consecrated to helping people who are hurting. That is why I have written all the books and poems and articles I have written.

When I lecture, I pray, "Let there be someone here who needs to hear what I have to say."

When I write, I pray, "May what I put down here lift the spirits of those who read it, give them hope and strength to meet what they have to meet, help them to keep faith and to find courage, help them above all to find meaning, for without meaning, what has any worth? To find meaning is to find God."

I have made this long digression, I suppose, to explain why I am making these lectures on reincarnation. I make them in the hope that they will help you to find meaning in what often appears to be a meaningless world.

So let me return to my vision of hell. I will give it here exactly as I wrote it for *Happi-*

ness Can Be a Habit, for that is how I experienced it.

Once I had a vision of hell.

As I was dragged past him down into the pit, I recognized Cerberus, the three-headed dog who guards the entrance, so I knew that it had to be hell.

But I could not believe it.

I showed such outrage and dismay that the demon who was dragging me was disturbed.

"It is not as bad as you think," he said. "You may not have to stay here long."

"I will not stay here long," I said. "I did not believe that God could make a place like this and I still cannot believe it. The maker of this place has only my hatred and contempt, and he will always have it. He will have to bind me and torture me. For I will fight against him with all my might and strength."

"You have the wrong idea about the place," said the demon, dragging me lower into the pit. "It is not like what you think it is at all. There is nobody here, you see, except those you feel ought to be here. Look around you."

I looked, and what the demon said was true. I could see nobody who I had not thought deserved to be in hell.

"Hell can only last as long as you feel it

should be here," the demon said.

The rest of my vision I cannot remember—whether I slunk down yet deeper into that pit of my shame and fear and hate, or whether in my unforgiveness I could not let hell go.

Heaven and hell are states in you and me. The gulf between them is no wider than a thought. I know people who spend every day in heaven and people who spend every day in hell.

If one morning you awoke feeling the way some people feel every morning, you would cry out, "I feel like hell." And if one morning you awoke feeling the way other people feel every morning, you would cry out, "What a heavenly morning! I've never felt this good before in all my life."

At every circle of hell I think I might find some human heart and I might find some human heart at every round of heaven.

Ah, yes, I believe in heaven and hell. I have known inhabitants of both these "countries", and I have spent some time in them myself.

But I don't believe in the traditional heaven and hell. I like the story about the couple who had a pact that if one of them passed on, they would try to get in touch on the anniversary of the passing. So on the anniversary of the husband's passing, the wife went into her room and sat there quietly in meditation. Finally, she heard a voice and she said, "Is this you, darling? Is this you?"

He said, "Yes, dear, this is I."

She said, "What's it like up there?"

"Oh, it's wonderful here, dear. Just wonderful. The sky is so blue and the grass is so green and the cows are so beautiful."

"Cows? I didn't know there were cows in heaven?"

"Heaven? Who said anything about heaven? I'm a bull in Montana."

Forgive me if my story shocks you. I don't mean it as fact. I mean it as humor. I mean it to make you laugh, and I hope it did. Laughter is a saving grace. I wish I could make these lectures humorous throughout, but I can't. The subject is not exactly humorous; but it's not the subject—it's me. I don't know that many funny stories.

In our time, many, many people—more I'm sure than ever before in human history—don't believe in an afterlife at all. They don't believe life has any meaning. It's just a gigantic accident. As I said, the discoveries of modern science have changed our ideas about the nature of things. Remember, until very recently we knew very little about the nature of the physical world in which we live, the structure of the universe. The earth was a vaguely flat area at the center of everything. The sun, the moon, and the stars came up out of the east, circled over us, and disappeared in the west. Heaven was located out beyond the stars; hell was located under the earth. God had created the earth the way the Bible tells us He did, and then He'd created us—in six days. We didn't know enough to have any reason to doubt it.

In fact, in the 1600s, an Irish archbishop named James Ussher—I think he figured it out by counting the chronologies in Genesis—wrote a paper showing that God had created the earth in 4,004 B.C. I'm not sure whether it was he or another theologian who announced that God not only did it in 4,004 B.C., but on the evening of Yom Kippur. I don't know how he arrived at the exact hour, but most people accepted his facts as factual. They didn't know anything that made them doubt it.

Oh, Copernicus and Galileo had upset the notion that the earth was the center of things, and had challenged the authority of the authoritative church. But it wasn't until the last century that enough scientific knowledge was accumulated to make it evident that the tales in the Bible that tell how the world and we humans beings came into being should not be considered as factual accounts, but have to be interpreted spiritually.

In 1833, Sir Charles Lyell completed his "The Principles of Geology" that showed that the earth was millions of years old. And then, in 1859, Charles Darwin wrote "Origin of Species" and advanced the theory of evolution. Religion has never been the same since. Science has revealed so many new truths about the world we live in and it has wrought so many miracles. It has changed the way we live in wonderful ways. It has done this just by dealing with physical laws and manipulating physical forces. It has done it without having to take any thought whatever of spiritual forces or of God. The result is, many people don't feel there's any reason to postulate the existence of a world beyond the physical world.

It is easy to see why so many scientists have taken an agnostic and even atheistic view of things. They have found that by investigating the nature of the material-physical world, and working with the principles they have found there, they can work miracles and uncover truths. The scientific mind is almost entirely occupied with analyzing material substances and observing physical events as the way to find out what the real facts about anything are. This is the scientific method, and the great success scientists have had with this method creates a natural bias; they are predisposed to assume that anything that cannot be explained in material-physical terms—that is, in what not only scientists but all of us have come to believe are scientific terms—is not real. Many scientists close their minds against even the possibility of paranormal occurrences.

Also, from the beginning of modern science, with Galileo, scientists have found organized religion arrayed against them and often doing all it could to hinder the advance of scientific knowledge. It has been natural for scientists, elated by their triumphs and feeling that religion did not wish them well, to shrug off religious beliefs as unnecessary, unreasonable, and impossible to validate.

However, it has been many years since some arrogant scientist has turned from dissecting a human body and scornfully exclaimed, "Where is the soul? I cannot find it anywhere!"

Science has matured to the point where it can question its own assumptions as well as those of religion, and scientists have discovered that there is more to life and more to creating the good life than finding natural laws and creating mechanical marvels. In the last few years, although more and more educated people have come to believe there is no world beyond the physical world or at least to have great doubts that there may be, science itself has begun to take an interesting twist. It has shown a growing interest in the paranormal—in such matters as extrasensory perception, in clairvoyance and telepathy, psychokinesis and levitation. In the past, reports of such occurrences have been simply shrugged off as impossible. Now, more and more scientists are beginning to look at these reports and ask, "Is it possible, Horatio, that there are more things in heaven and earth than are dreamt of in our philosophy?" Can these reports have validity?

More and more scientists have begun to explore the notion that mind is just as real as matter; the world of the mind is just as real as the physical world; and events may occur that cannot be explained in physical terms but are just as real as those that can.

Naturally, I'm delighted to see science taking this turn. I believe in the reality of mind. I believe in God. I believe we are spiritual beings, and denying the spiritual part of our nature will bring about just as dire results as denying the physical part of our being.

It's interesting, isn't it, that at the same time more and more people are losing faith in the probability of a spiritual world, more and more scientists are becoming interested in the possibility that there is such a world. We have a wave of parapsychological investigations going on in scientific laboratories. I believe the reason for this apparent contradiction is that people have not lost faith in a spiritual world; they have just lost faith in the kind of spiritual world the traditional churches have tried to make us believe in, the quasi-physical kind with eternal heavens and hells and devils and judgment days and the like in it. We want to believe, but we can't believe what our reason requires us to reject. So, we have all this parapsychological investigation going on.

As for myself, I am certain that there are phenomena we can only describe as mental or even supernatural. They have no explanation in physical terms, and I don't think we're ever going to find a physical explanation. I've had a number of experiences that convince me—yes, completely convince me—that there are forces in the world besides physical ones, and that events occur that can't be explained merely in physical terms.

I have never sought such experiences. As a matter of fact, I have been afraid of them. I have known a number of persons who did seek them and became so involved in their pursuit that they lost touch with the world of sense and senses in which we all find ourselves and in which we all have to live, and live effectively.

So I have never sought such experiences, but as I say, they have occasionally come to me. At this point let me relate just one.

Almost forty years ago my first wife died. One day, in the midst of happy circumstances, she complained of pain. I took her to the doctor. He insisted on an immediate operation. He came out of the operating room and told me that the operation was of no avail, a malignancy had spread throughout her body, and at best she had a few months to live.

You can imagine my mental state; I was stricken. I did not know what to do. I did not feel that I could tell anyone what was my wife's condition, as I was afraid she might find out and I did not want that to happen. At least not immediately.

On the day after the operation, I was called to a telephone. My mother was on the line. "Jim," she said, "what is wrong with you?"

My mother lived more than a thousand miles away. She had lived there twelve years. In all that time, she had never called me, not once.

I had not told my mother that my wife was ill. She had no way of knowing. The conversation showed me that she didn't know; it was me she was concerned about.

"All day," my mother said, "I've had a dreadful sense there is something terribly wrong with you. I called Unity School (where I worked; I had told no one there the doctor's verdict) and they told me you were at the hospital. What is wrong with you?"

Now you may say that this experience is merely a coincidence. There is no way to prove that it is not. But if ever I have had a need of coincidence, I needed it that day!

I will, of course, never believe it was a coincidence. If it was, coincidence must be another name for miracle. To me it was like the brush of angel wings. I do not believe you can have such an experience and not believe that we are more than we seem to be, and there is more to the world than can be explained in physical terms.

The fact is, no one can really believe he's just a mechanism. No one. I can believe you are, but I can't believe I am. Think about that, and you'll see how true it is. It is psychologically impossible for you to believe you are a machine, however much you may theorize about it, however much you may say you accept a mechanistic, materialistic, naturalistic philosophy.

I would accept such a philosophy, however, if my only alternative were to believe, as some churches do, that this little life is the only life we have, and then on the basis of how we live this one life we are judged for eternity. Rather than believe that, I would agree with the materialists—the world is merely a gigantic and meaningless accident— there's no way so unfair a world could possibly be the work of a God. As I say, I've written books, articles, poems on this subject.

If there is a God, He has to be Intelligence. He has to be Justice and Order. I think He even has to be Love. There's no way Intelligence and Justice and Order and Love could make us to live this one life and then judge us for eternity on how we managed to live it. Such a world is too unfair a world!

Consider two children. One of them is born into a rich family, a happy family, a harmonious family. He's brought up in a secure world. He gets a good education. He marries. He has happy children of his own. He has good health all his life, or most of it, and at sixty, seventy, or eighty, he dies peacefully in bed.

Another child is born ill, half-starved, maimed in body and mind. Maybe he lives for minutes—or maybe for hours or months or a few years. He's abused all that time, twisted in mind, taught to rob and kill—or maybe he's brought up in a savage world of civil war and trouble and is murdered in his youth.

That one of these two turns out to be a moral, law-abiding citizen, and the other turns out to be a thief and a murderer cannot possibly provide a basis for eternal judgment.

Our human world is filled with such differences of birth, and life, and death as these. We see them all the time and everywhere. If there is a God, there has to be an explanation for such injustices. The world where this little life we see is all the life we have, and we're born into it in such unequal conditions, such a world *cannot* be the work of a God—it's too unfair!

No, if there is a God, two things have to be true:

One—I am an immortal being.

Two—I draw my own life to me.

If there is a God, and this world is His work, these two things must be true.

Let's consider the first item. Are we immortal? By immortal, I mean we lived before we were born and will live after we die. As I say, in our time, many question this. But let's consider the question and I think we will see there are a number of convincing reasons to believe in our immortality.

First, there is a scientific reason, drawn from the physical world.

In the physical world there is a law called the Law of the Conservation of Energy, the First Law of Thermodynamics. In all of science there is no principle more important, more universally accepted by scientists. It is the common principle of all the natural sciences. It is usually expressed by saying that when energy is destroyed in one form, it appears in a corresponding quantity in another form. In other words, in the physical world, nothing disappears except to reappear in another form; nothing is eliminated. Things change from one form to another. That is all. Things change.

Is it not reasonable to believe, if this is true of my physical components, it is also true of me and of my mind and soul? I change. My mind and soul change. But we don't cease to be. This is the first law of science: though all things change, nothing perishes. And it's not only scientists who affirm this truth. Look about you. In all the world around you, do you not see everywhere a principle of recurrence?

A second reason to believe I am immortal is that to live well, I have to live as if I am immortal. I wrote a poem about it once. I am not going to read it to you, but it starts off: *I am immortal, I aver, for I must live as if I were.* And that's a very, very true statement.

Once the few physical needs of the body are taken care of, we give most of our time and energy to satisfying needs and hungers that have little relation to our physical nature. If the physical creature is all we are, is it not strange that such an important part of our life should be what goes on in our mind, that our greatest hungers are inward hungers, that our greatest needs are needs of the spirit?

If this life were all the life we had, self-preservation and pleasure would be our only motivation. But that's not the way it is. Oh, this life is very good—we should try to live it as long as we can, and we should value its pleasures—I want all the life and pleasure I can get. But merely holding on to life, merely holding on to pleasure has never been considered our highest good. Look how cheaply some people hold life. Sometimes this scares us, sometimes it awes us. People die for so many things, and they die so readily, so easily for them. They die for love of country— think of all the people who have done that. They die for pride's sake. They die from disappointment. They die for love. They'd rather lose their life than lose their self-respect; they'd rather lose their life than lose the respect of other people. They die rather than be false to what they believe to be true. The Christian martyrs did that, and people are still doing it. The interesting thing is that it isn't the worst human beings who hold life so lightly. It's the very best human beings, the very strongest, the very bravest, the very wisest. It's Socrates saying to his judges: *"The difficulty, my friends, is not in avoiding death, but in avoiding unrighteousness, for that runs faster than death."* And the greatest man of all saying: *"Father . . . remove this cup from me; nevertheless not my will, but thine, be done."* (Luke 22:42) I feel there is some part of us that knows with Krishna, as he says in the Bhagavad Gita: *If the slayer thinks he slays, or if the slain thinks he is slain, neither of these knows the truth about himself. For the Self is never born and never dies.* There is some part of us that knows this. It's why human beings can do all these self-sacrificing acts, and do them with such grace. For this we do.

We feel in our bones that we are immortal. Karl Menninger, the psychiatrist, says, *"No human being can, in the deepest core of his being, conceive of non-existence or imagine it occurring to him."* I think you will see how true that is if you'll think about how you feel about yourself.

There is a bit of clever verse called "Ben Karshook's Wisdom"—I don't know who wrote it.

Quoth a young Sadducee,
"Reader of many rolls,
Is it so certain we
Have, as they tell us, souls?"

"Son, there is no reply!"
The Rabbi bit his beard.
"Certain a soul have I—
We* may have none," he sneered.*

Yet one more reason why I believe we are immortal is, there's a great deal of evidence that we're immortal, a great deal. Now, it's not complete evidence—the scientific laboratory kind—because it's usually personal, very personal. But there are all kinds of reports, and there have been for thousands of years, from people who have said, "I communed with the dead." The interesting thing about this is, if you've ever had an experience like it, you find that it's very difficult to communicate it to anybody else. But it's the most real experience you'll ever have in your life. If you have such an experience, it's so real you cannot doubt it. Yet when you try to tell it to somebody else, it kind of dissipates, and you can almost see people saying, "Oh, that's something he dreamed, something he thought up, something he needed to believe." Maybe you have had such an experience. Most people have had some kind of experiences that are not explainable in physical terms. If you have, you know how real it is—and how hard it is to communicate its reality.

During the last few years there have appeared in books and magazines a number of reports of what the writers have called near-death experiences. Dr. Elizabeth Kubler-Ross, Dr. Raymond Moody, Kenneth Ring, and others have written about these incidents. People have died. Yes, technically, at least, they were dead; in many of these incidents they've been pronounced dead by attending physicians. But they came back to life and then related their experience, and there's no question, all who have had this experience are convinced there is another life. They believe beyond question—they've had a brief experience in this other life.

One thing about these near-death reports that I've liked—they report there is nothing to fear. Personally, I've always felt there is nothing to fear. Their experience was universally a kindly one. None of them reports anything that looks like the traditional heaven or hell.

I think deep down we all sense that there is

nothing to fear. Nobody has ever really believed in hell. Not for himself. He may have said he did. He may have had some kind of theological belief in it, but he did not really believe in it—not in his heart—not in the essential fibers of his being. Had men really believed in hell, think how different history would have been. Who would cheat, rob, murder, if he really believed he will inescapably be punished with incessant and everlasting pain. No! We'd all be living lives of perfect love—or if we weren't capable of that, we'd at least be law-abiding—if we really believed that.

There's a humorous old German epigram about heaven and hell. It shows how lightly people have always taken them: *Himmel für Klima; Hölle für Gesellschaft.* (Heaven for climate; Hell for society.)

But I've gotten off the subject of the evidence for another life. Let's look at it. On the one hand, we have all this evidence—the reports of thousands upon thousands of people who say, "I communicated with the dead." This may not be laboratory evidence, but neither is it contrived. If you have had such an experience, I don't have to tell you how real, how convincing it is.

On the other hand, what evidence do we have that there's not a life after death? There's not one shred that there's not another life. Have you ever realized that? How can there be? It would be impossible to collect and even more impossible to report. If there isn't another life, nobody's been there to know there isn't and he can't report back because he no longer is. So you have a lot of evidence on the positive side—none on the negative side.

It may be that we believe there's life after death—partly, at least, but only partly—because we want to believe in it. But belief aside, there is all this evidence; much of it stories and reports by individuals that cannot be checked, but very vivid stories and reports of experiences so vivid they leave no doubt in the minds of those who have them. On the other hand, those who believe there is no life after death must believe this wholly out of their desire to believe it, wholly because they want to believe it, because there is not one shred of evidence to support their belief. There cannot be.

One of the main reasons I've chosen to make these talks about reincarnation is because I'm a believer. I believe there is a God, and I believe life has meaning. But to believe in Him, I have to find a reasonable way to explain how life can be the way we see it lived—its injustices, its cruelties, its heroes, its saints, and alas, its many villains—and be His work. The only reasonable way I can explain this, unless I believe the whole thing has no meaning and is an accident, is to believe in reincarnation. I am what I am because I grew to be this in former existences; and I will go on after death into further existences. In my case, because I believe in God and believe that He's love and intelligence, I also believe I'm growing to be the spiritual being He made me to be. I have lived before and I will live again. My life is what it is now because of what I was in former lives, and my future life will be what it will be because of what I am now. This is what I believe. To me it's the only way you can make this life make sense; otherwise, the whole affair is a meaningless mishmash of chance and ill-chance, where physical beings, lucky and unlucky enough to be born in the physical environment they find themselves in, are doomed to live out their short or long lives as physical forces—the so-called laws of nature—may decree.

I don't like the word *reincarnation* because it causes people to reject the idea. The moment you talk to the average American and say reincarnation, you can almost see him shutting you off. But any other word that describes it is equally unfortunate, even worse. Metempsychosis, palingenesis, re-embodiment, rebirth, transmigration, and the like—they're no improvement. With most of the words, the moment you say them, people call up occult images and strange religions. We've been programmed against them.

I had this experience many years ago with a nun. I decided I'd like to learn French. I knew French, but I didn't know it well. There happens to be a French convent in Kansas City—Notre Dame de Sion. So I went out and knocked on the door and said that I'd like to learn French.

I then had this nun, a lovely human being, very very bright, she had graduated from the Sorbonne, and she and I had this French class. It was a private class, though my wife always had to be there because the nun wasn't allowed to be alone with me. I don't know whether they didn't trust me or the nun! But we both enjoyed it. The conversation was always in French—she never spoke

English to me—she could, but she refused to do it. If you're going to learn French, you learn it in French. So, I had to try to talk French with her, if I was going to talk.

I would bring her Unity pamphlets—she asked me to bring them—and we would have tremendous arguments over religion. She always won them because they were in French and she could speak it so much better than I. One time my wife decided we were both getting too loud and excited, and she signaled me to stop—and the nun turned to her and said, "Leave him alone. I like it."

I brought her a pamphlet, Charles Fillmore's pamphlet on reincarnation, "Preserving the Unity of Soul and Body." I gave her that, and the next class she was waiting for me. "How could you possibly believe anything of this sort?"

So I said, "What do you believe? Do you believe you are going to heaven and sit on a cloud there and play on a harp?"

She said, "Of course, I don't believe anything like that! I believe that life is a process. Life is a progress."

I said, "Then you believe exactly what I believe, except you don't like the word. It's just the word you're rejecting, not the idea." And

48

I think if you talk to most people, that's what you'd find.

So as I say, I don't like the word, because it turns people off—we've been programmed against it by fifteen hundred years of teaching in the Christian world, that reincarnation is a strange and spooky teaching that only a few people believe in—people who live in far-off parts of the world—Hindus mainly, and ignorant, of course—people who believe in all kinds of occult and exotic beliefs.

But reincarnation is the word we have. One dictionary says it means, *"rebirth in new bodies or forms of life; especially rebirth of a soul in a new human body."* That's a pretty clear and straight-forward meaning for a word to have. So I present *The Case for Reincarnation.*

The Bible, the Church,
and Reincarnation

Before I go further, thinking about my discussion with the nun and how we have been programmed against the idea of reincarnation, I'd like to discuss reincarnation and the Bible, and also the history of reincarnation in the Christian church. We live in a Christian world, a world that has a high regard for the Bible. And many people are concerned because there seems to be no definite reference to reincarnation in the Bible. It's true that the word *reincarnation* does not appear there, and it's also true that for hundreds of years reincarnation has had no place in orthodox Christian doctrine. Most Christian churches think of reincarnation in negative terms. So I thought we should consider—

What is the teaching of the Western World, the Jewish-Christian world, about the afterlife, and how did Christian doctrine form on this subject?

Of course, we know the general Christian belief today is that if you believe in Jesus Christ and you're good, your soul will be taken to heaven when you die. Heaven is a very pleasant place. If you don't believe in Jesus Christ, and you are bad, you will go to hell, a fiery place down below. If you're a Catholic, you believe you've got a chance to go to purgatory. Heaven, hell, purgatory—this is the official doctrine, though I wonder how many people really believe this sort of thing anymore. Certainly many do not; it is too implausible.

It's true that there are few references that can be related to reincarnation in the Bible, very few. But there aren't many references in the Bible about heaven and hell. Most of them about heaven—especially the ones where Jesus talks about it—would indicate that He was not thinking of a place in the sky, but of a state within. He said to His disciples: "... *nor will they say, 'Lo, here it is!' or 'There!' for behold, the kingdom of God is in the midst of you*" (Luke 17:21). When they pressed Him to tell them about heaven, He likened it to a little leaven and a mustard seed and a pearl of great price. That does not sound as if He was pointing to a city on a celestial map.

The Greek word in the New Testament that we translate as heaven is *ouranos,* and what it really means is a state of expanded consciousness—that makes sense. That's not a geographical, but a metaphysical way to think about heaven.

Jesus was a little more graphic about hell, but even there everything we know about Jesus indicates that He was describing states of consciousness, not geographical locations. Jesus taught principles. He tried to get people to change their hearts and minds, their way of life, and He taught mainly in symbols.

There is no reference to purgatory in the Bible. None.

There are a dozen or more places in the Bible where, if you believe in reincarnation, you might reasonably say, "I think the man who wrote this was making a reference to reincarnation." There are a few places in the Bible where you have to be completely opposed to reincarnation to believe that the writer meant anything but reincarnation.

The Bible is not the simplest, clearest work in the world. If you've read much of it, you realize that. Remember, in the form we get it, in English, it's a translation of a translation of a translation. There are hundreds of sects, cults, denominations, and churches in the world, and all of them interpret the Bible as saying whatever they want it to say. When some sect claims it accepts the Bible literally, that just means it accepts literally those parts of the Bible that agree with what it wishes to teach, and pays no attention to the parts that don't agree with it.

For myself, I've not found the Bible easy to understand. Maybe you do. But it's often very hard for me to know just what the writer was trying to say, especially writers like Paul and some of the prophets. However, I appreciate Mark Twain's feeling. He said it wasn't the parts of the Bible he didn't understand that troubled him, it was the parts he did understand.

Historically, the Catholics have thought the Bible so difficult to understand that for hundreds of years they forbade Catholics to read it. It's only been recently that Catholics have been allowed to read it, and I don't think it's recommended yet. You weren't supposed to read the book because the church fathers didn't think you were going to get anything of value out of reading it. In fact, you were likely to get mixed up. You would be wiser to leave it to the priest to tell you what it means.

I'd like to read you a few passages from the Bible that I think clearly point to a belief in reincarnation. The version of the Bible I have used is the Revised Standard Version, published in 1952. There are many versions of the Bible; they differ. Scholars have long realized that most of the versions we have in English, especially the King James, are filled with errors. This Revised Standard Version is the work of many Bible scholars from many different churches, and is generally accepted as the most accurate we have. The passages I quote from are not substantially different in earlier versions.

Amazingly, the best of these passages that suggest reincarnation consist of statements made by Jesus, or they describe incidents in which He took part.

The Old Testament had predicted that Elijah would return before the appearance of the Messiah and the end of the world. A part of the very last statement in the Old Testament is this one in Malachi: *"Behold, I will send you Elijah the prophet before the great and terrible day of the Lord comes."*

At Jesus' transfiguration, He took Peter and James and John up with Him into the mountain and there He appeared to them in glory with Moses and Elijah. Afterward: *... as they were coming down the mountain, Jesus commanded them, "Tell no one the vision, until the Son of man is raised from the dead." And the disciples asked him, "Then why do the scribes say that first Elijah must come?" He replied, "Elijah does come, and he is to restore all things; but I tell you that Elijah has already come, and they did not know him, but did to him whatever they pleased. So also the Son of man will suffer at their hands." Then the disciples understood that he was speaking to them of John the Baptist* (Matt. 17:9-13).

In another place in Matthew, He said: *"Truly, I say to you, among those born of women there has risen no one greater than John the Baptist... and if you are willing to accept it, he is Elijah who is to come. He who has ears to hear, let him hear"* (Matt. 11:11-15).

Now John's own comment about who he

was is very interesting, at least to me, and very hard to explain except in terms of reincarnation if you accept Jesus' statement that John was Elijah: ... *when the Jews sent priests and Levites from Jerusalem to ask him, "Who are you?" he said, "I am not the Christ." And they asked him, "What then? Are you Elijah?" He said, "I am not." "Are you the prophet?" And he answered, "No." They said to him then, "Who are you? ... What do you say about yourself?" He said, "I am the voice of one crying in the wilderness ..."* (John 1:19-23).

John's comments are just what you would expect if you believe in reincarnation. If we do reincarnate, obviously most of us don't remember who we were. John didn't remember being anyone but John.

These statements of Jesus and John sound a lot like they were talking about reincarnation. In fact, it's hard to believe they weren't. These statements make Jesus Himself an authority for it. "John is Elijah," He essentially said. And He added, "If you are willing to accept it ... He who has ears to hear, let him hear." His comments indicate that He knew many people would not accept His statement that John is Elijah, which is true; a lot of people didn't believe in reincarnation then, just as they don't now. The first Christians were divided as to their belief in reincarnation, but the priests and bishops who gained power to determine what the doctrine was to be decided against it.

These statements of Jesus, of course, had gotten into the Bible. Those who have not believed in reincarnation have handled them simply by denying that they mean what they seem to mean. They have said, "Jesus didn't mean what He was saying. He was talking in symbolic language; He merely meant that John was like Elijah. It couldn't be true that Jesus meant literally what He said. Elijah couldn't have reincarnated as John because he never died. He was transported to heaven in a chariot of fire."

But Jesus and the disciples clearly believed Elijah had come back, and Jesus identified him as John. If the relationship between Elijah and John wasn't by way of reincarnation because Elijah hadn't died but had been transported to heaven in a chariot of fire, why didn't he come back in a chariot of fire?

John was born in a completely natural way to Elizabeth; there is a very elaborate account of his conception and birth in Luke.

John himself had no memory of being Elijah. If Elijah had just come hot-rodding back from heaven, I think he would have had at least some idea of who he was. You would, wouldn't you? But John didn't know, which would have been the usual case had he been reincarnated, because that's how it is with us.

One thing certain, Jesus said, "John is Elijah." It's a very hard-to-explain incident if Jesus and His disciples didn't believe in reincarnation.

The most conclusive incident of all is the well-known story in John, where Jesus heals the man born blind from birth: ... *his disciples asked him, "Rabbi, who sinned, this man or his parents, that he was born blind?" Jesus answered, "It was not that this man sinned, or his parents, but that the works of God might be made manifest in him"* (John 9:2, 3).

Obviously, the idea that the man might have sinned before he was born was not an idea strange or unacceptable to Jesus or to His disciples. None of them said, "Oh, that would be impossible. The man wasn't there before he was born." There must have been an acceptance of preexistence for this man or they would never have asked Jesus this question. Or, Jesus would have said, "What do you mean, before he was born?" or something like that. The only way you could sin before you were born is that you were alive before you were born. Only that would make it possible for you to sin. But to be alive before you were born, you must have had a former existence and been reincarnated. Jesus clearly considered this to be a possible explanation for the man's being born blind, for He said, "It was not that this man sinned." In other words, "No, in this case, what the man had done in his former life was not the cause of his blindness."

There are a dozen or so other passages in the Old and New Testaments that may allude to reincarnation, but they can be interpreted in different ways. This is from Jeremiah, the first chapter: *Now the word of the Lord came to me saying, "Before I formed you in the womb I knew you, and before you were born I consecrated you; I appointed you a prophet to the nations."*

Then I said, "Ah, Lord God! Behold, I do not know how to speak, for I am only a youth." But the Lord said to me,

"Do not say, 'I am only a youth'; for to all to whom I send you you shall go, and what-

ever I command you you shall speak" (Jer. 1:4-7).

But those instances with Jesus and His disciples prove to me that they were familiar with the belief and they did not repudiate it. Neither did the early Christians.

But reincarnation did not have a happy history in the Christian church. There are good reasons for this. To understand what happened, let's examine the beliefs about the afterlife and the next world that existed in the time of Jesus.

First, all ancient people had hazy notions about the next life, nothing definite. Don't we still? But most people believed in it, in the same uncertain way we do. Few of them thought you were going to die and that was the end of you. That is true of all ancient people.

But their view of the next world was a ghostly one. The ghostly dead, good and bad alike, wandered like vaporous mists through a vaporous mist. Achilles, the greatest of Greek heroes, met Ulysses at the gates of hell and described his existence there in gloomy terms as a nebulous nothingness. The Greeks had a saying, "Better to be the meanest slave on earth than to be the shade of Achilles."

The Jewish people had extremely hazy beliefs about the next life. Judaism is a this-world religion. The Old Testament makes few definite statements as to what's going to happen after you die. I believe it was trying to teach us that we had better make the best of it right here. The "History of Religions" by George Foote Moore is probably the most scholarly work on world religions yet published. It says of the early Jewish belief about the dead:

The lot of the shades is miserable, deprived of life and the joy of living, inhabiting the tomb or the dark recesses of the earth. In the nether world itself there is no separation of good and bad; nor have the great of the earth a prospect of brighter fortune in the company of the gods, as they have in Egypt or in the Elysium of the Greeks. These early notions remained substantially unchanged until the last centuries before the Christian era.

If you look to the Bible, you find in Ecclesiastes: *The fate of the sons of men and the fate of beasts is the same; as one dies, so dies the other. . . . All go to one place; all are from the dust, and all turn to dust again. Who knows whether the spirit of man goes upward and the spirit of the beast goes down to the earth?* (Eccles. 3:19-21).

And Job in his fourteenth chapter says: *"There is hope for a tree, if it be cut down, that it will sprout again .... But man dies ... and where is he? As waters fail from a lake, and a river wastes away and dries up, so man lies down and rises not again"* (Job 14:7-11).

You might think from these quotations from the Bible that some of the writers of the book did not believe in an afterlife at all. That could be. There have been individuals in every age who had doubts.

By the time Jesus lived, the Jewish people had a number of beliefs about the next world. The Sadducees—mainly the priests and upper class members of society—still held for the most part to the gloomy belief that you went into the pit—Sheol—and that was it. The Essenes, a mystical community that lived by the Dead Sea, the people who preserved the Dead Sea Scrolls for us, these Essenes believed in reincarnation. There are legends that Jesus in His youth lived with the Essenes.

The Pharisees were the largest group. While they, too, believed in reincarnation, they also had a belief in the afterworld of heaven and hell, angels and demons we are familiar with. They probably brought it back from their captivity in Persia. The Persians had been relatively kind masters, and the Jewish people liked them. I've read somewhere that the Persians are the only foreign people for whom the Bible has a friendly word. Isaiah called Cyrus, the Persian emperor, "the anointed" of the Lord, and the Magi, who were Persian priests, attended Jesus' birth.

The influence of the ancient Persian religion, Zoroastrianism, is interesting. Today relatively few Zoroastrians remain—mainly the Parsees in India. But their eschatology—that's a big word theologians like to use, meaning their ideas about the afterworld, their beliefs about what happens after death, their vision of the future and final fate of the world—this has greatly affected all of us.

The Jews brought it back from their captivity in Persia. Then Christianity, naturally, developed its notions from the Jewish belief, and Mohammed, seven centuries later, got his notions of the afterlife from his association with Jewish rabbis and Christian and Zoroastrian teachers and missionaries who wandered about the Arabian deserts.

Consider what the Persians believed and compare it with Christian orthodoxy. They called their God Ahura Mazda—a lovely name—it means simply "Wise Lord" (Edison named his newly invented light bulb after him). Ahura Mazda is the Good Lord, the divine creator who made heaven and earth. But he's opposed by the devil. The Persian name for the devil is *Ahriman*, but he's the leader of the Daevas, which we sometimes spell d-e-v-i. D-e-v-i is remarkably close to d-e-v-i-l. The name *Satan* comes from Shaitan. It was an old Semitic term for the evil jinn. The jinn (we're more likely to say genie)— remember Aladdin's lamp—the jinn were invisible spirits that lurked in hidden places, ready to appear in human or animal form and do you good or harm. Most Mideastern people believed in them.

The devil got his traditional shape, however, not from Persia, but from Greece. He looks remarkably like Pan, if you give Pan's face a malicious touch. Pan was a very popular god of shepherds and hunters, fields and forests, and the early Church might well have disposed of him by turning him into the devil. Milton in "Paradise Lost" named the central hall of hell *Pandemonium*. The church fathers were intelligent and practical men; they had a knack for turning popular gods and goddesses into demons—or saints!

But let's go back to the Persians.

The Persians had heaven—even one of our favorite names for heaven—Paradise—that's a Persian word. They had hell—though we get our classic description of this place from Dante, who got his more from the Greeks and Romans than the Persians—the Roman poet Vergil took him on the infernal tour. The Persians even had a border state—purgatory?—for those not really wicked enough for hell but not holy enough for heaven.

I believe scholars are agreed, the Jews brought back their array of angels and archangels from Persia. For example, the Persians had an angel just like Gabriel, only he had a different name, I think it was Israfel; he will blow his trumpet and all the dead will rise. When he does—oh, ultimate Christian orthodoxy of Christian orthodoxy, except that it's Persian—the earth will be asked to give up our bones, the water will give up our blood, the grass will give up our hair, and the fire will give up our life; and our body will be reconstituted of its original materials. Believe it or not!

As I say, we got the whole works, even including the virgin birth of Jesus, from the Zoroastrians. The Persians had three messiahs, all born of virgins, each 1,000 years after the other. We get the idea of the millennium from them, too. The third millennium will end with Gabriel's—I mean Israfel's—trumpet and Judgment Day. But the Persian notion is kinder than the Christian one. Hell doesn't go on forever. It just goes on to the end of the age. At the end of the age, when Gabriel-Israfel blows his trumpet, the world will end—in fire, of course. The fire will burn the wickedness out of us—painfully but quickly—and after that we'll all share in salvation. Many Christian thinkers believe that our idea of an eternal hell was mistakenly imposed on us when early translators used words like *everlasting* and *forever,* where the original authors of the Bible had meant the end of the age. In fact, in some modern versions of the Bible, this phrase is used again.

One item we didn't take in detail from the Persians is Zoroaster's description of what happens to you immediately after you die, but I think I ought to give it because I think you'll find it interesting and also because it's still very much alive in the world. The Moslems took it in full detail and it is part of Moslem belief today. The Moslems took Zoroaster's hell, too,—oh, just as hot as ours, but mainly an inky, stinky place—utterly foul and utterly dark—so dark that though hell is packed with the wicked, no one can see anyone else, so each one feels that he is alone. That's not a bad idea about hell. I wrote a poem about this in one of my books.

Some have thought hell to be fire,
but others have said
hell is an inky blackness
into which we are plunged alone.
In such a state
even a demon coming to torment us
would be welcome.

Has not despair the quality of emptiness?
To listen but not to hear,
to look but not to see,
to reach but not to touch—if I had to draw it,
would I not draw empty space
and in it
nothing
but me!

And to turn it into love,
I would need to add
only the lightest brush
of fingertips!

But to return to what the Zoroastrians and now the Moslems also believe happens when you die—for three days your soul lingers in your body while you review your life. I think some Christians believe this. If you're good, after three blissful days, on the fourth day a perfumed breeze appears and a beautiful maiden, the embodiment of your goodness, conducts you to the Cinvat Bridge. If you were wicked, after three days of distress, a foul stench appears, and a hideous hag, the embodiment of your evil ways, conducts you to the Cinvat Bridge. This bridge is a gigantic shining sword that spans the abyss of hell. Good or bad you must step out on the Cinvat Bridge. If you're good, the wide flat of the blade will present itself to you, and you cross into heaven. If you're bad, the razor sharp edge of the blade presents itself and you plunge into hell.

But so much for Zoroastrian, Moslem, and Christian eschatology.

One important item we should keep in mind

as we think about the relationship of reincarnation and Christianity—many of us have the notion that immediately after Jesus' death the Christian religion sprang into being exactly as it is now. That isn't the case at all.

The teachings that are taught as Christianity by the various churches today did not spring verbatim from the words of Jesus, who wrote nothing, or even from the words that after many years got written down as His words. The New Testament, as we have it today, is a collection of stories and essays, which were written down years after His death, some of them perhaps a century later. Hundreds of stories and essays were written and rewritten in the centuries after His death, all claiming to be genuine revelations about His life and teachings. Slowly over the years some of these pieces came to be accepted as authentic by most of those who called themselves Christians. These included the Four Gospels, though John had trouble being accepted, most of Paul's Epistles, and Acts.

It was only after four hundred years of violent argument that the bishops were able to settle on twenty-seven pieces of writing— our present New Testament—and declare that these and only these were to be accepted as genuine revelations.

The Catholic Bible has always included a number of books in the Old Testament that the Protestant Bible does not include, and during the Reformation there was much question as to what books should be included; Luther, for instance, rejected James, Hebrews, Jude, and Revelation.

If you are a member of a Christian church, you have only to consider the origin of your own version of Christianity to see that Christianity did not appear suddenly complete two thousand years ago in the fields of Palestine. It took the Catholic Church hundreds of years and much violent argument to develop its version of Christianity. If you are a Protestant, how old is your version? Even if you are a Hussite or a Lutheran, it is hardly older than five hundred years.

For a long time after Jesus' death, there was no established Christian doctrine. There were all kinds of beliefs. Anybody could get up in a church and say, "I just had a revelation. God spoke to me, and this is what He told me." And that's what people did. Hundreds of different Christian cults appeared.

But after several centuries of this, the

bishops said, "If any revelations are going to be made, from now on they're only going to be made to us bishops." That stopped the revelations. Somehow bishops haven't been a very inspired lot. But that didn't establish an agreed-upon doctrine.

Each bishop wanted everyone to believe what he believed. We all do, don't we? So they fought about what was to be the doctrine. Bishops fought bishops, and they were a jealous, ambitious lot. Slowly, only after hundreds of years, after many councils and many battles, the Catholic Church, with its bishop the Pope, became dominant.

But remember, many Christians never accepted the doctrines the Roman Catholic Church put forth. Never. They haven't to this day. There are still a great number of great churches that do not accept the rule of the papacy, including, of course, all Protestants. But even from the beginning they didn't. The Nestorians, the Monophysites, the Greek Eastern Church—these are as old as the Roman Catholic Church. And in the Catholic Church itself, the official doctrine has changed many times.

It is not surprising that Christianity became what it was in the early Church; it would have been surprising if it had not. Ancient religion was mainly a matter of rituals and ceremonies, of sacraments and sacrifices, of priests and temples.

This was especially true in Rome. The Romans were busily occupied conquering the world, and to be sure that their relations with the other world were not bungled, they turned religion over to experts; the Roman priests ran it on a *quid pro quo* basis, where if you fulfilled your part, the gods fulfilled theirs.

I have always liked the story of how Julius Caesar in Gaul, as he debated whether to cross the Rubicon and return to Rome, sent priests scurrying through the camp to find a chicken whose entrails would provide him the right go-ahead sign.

A religion of priests and rituals was the only religion most people knew. They were not prepared for a religion that put the responsibility for their spiritual welfare on themselves, and they would not have wanted one. So it is not surprising that Christianity remained largely a religion of rituals conducted by priests, with a supreme pontiff, the pontifex maximus, still at their head.

I don't mean to say that Christianity did

not change things. It changed things profoundly, for it brought a number of fundamental changes to people's beliefs.

For one thing, it eliminated sacrifice, Jesus Himself becoming the sacrifice. For another, it presented His ethical teachings and asked people to live by much higher moral standards than they had before. Perhaps most important of all, it gave them the story of Jesus' life, death, and resurrection. The belief in an afterlife in Jesus' time was mainly of a dim and spectral existence, a thing of ghosts and tombs. Christianity gave people hope that they, too, might be resurrected and have another life after this one, a better life. Christians expected the world to end in their lifetime. Gabriel was going to blow his horn; Jesus was coming back in a cloud of glory; and those who were alive would live on and the dead would be re-embodied and they would all be happy, contented citizens in the New Jerusalem, the kingdom of heaven on earth. Their old enemies, of course, would all be in hell.

I'm sorry to report this—it's a sad commentary on the influence of religion—but as I have said, there seem to be a lot of people who enjoy the idea of people, other people, burning in hell. The early church fathers wrote some vivid accounts of what a joy it was going to be to sit up in heaven and listen to the howling down below. Tertullian, one of the most famous of the early Christian writers had this to say:

How vast the spectacle will be on that day. How I shall marvel, laugh, rejoice, and exalt seeing so many kings, supposedly received into heaven, groaning in the depths of darkness. And the magistrates who persecuted the name of Jesus melting in fiercer flames than they ever kindled against the Christians. Sages and philosophers blushing before their disciples as they blaze together, players lighter of limb by far in the fire, and charioteers burning red on the wheel of flame.

These were not very kindly times. I don't know that we've gotten much kinder, but I think a little. As I say, a lot of people are still looking forward to hell—for others, that is.

It was two or three hundred years before most Christians realized the world was not about to end. A lot of people still believe it is, don't they? Just about every year somebody manages to collect a band of people and off they go down into the desert or up into the hills, or somewhere, and wait for the world to end. Of course, it hasn't yet. Personally, I don't think it's going to end for a long, long time. But then I don't believe in the Judgment Day, when Gabriel will blow his horn. I feel like the Irish lad who stopped the priest who had just delivered a sermon about Judgment Day and said, "Father, I'd like to ask you a question about this Judgment Day you were talking about. Is that for everybody?"

"Everybody, my son."

"You mean all the people in the world are going to be there, all assembled together in one place, when that day comes?"

"Yes, my son."

"The Arabs and the Jews?"

"Yes, my son."

"The Irish and the English?"

"Yes, my son."

"The Catholics and the Protestants?"

"Yes, my son."

"Well, Father, there's going to be darn little judging on that day."

Somehow most of us have the notion that always, from its very beginning, Christianity rejected reincarnation. Nothing could be further from the truth. In the early days of Christianity, there were many who believed in it. There was nothing in the teachings of

Jesus that excluded the belief in reincarnation. It is not hard to see, however, why the Church, as it was deciding what its teaching should be, in the waning years of the Roman Empire, from the third to the sixth century A.D., decided against reincarnation. For one thing, the belief grew that the Church itself had the power to determine what your next life would be—this had to be extremely appealing to the Church. For another thing, there was certainly no popular demand for reincarnation. Consider what life was like. The thought of having to come back and live it again could not have appealed to many.

There were little law and order in the Roman Empire. There was almost continual war. War, starvation, poverty, and pestilence kept the average life expectancy at about twenty years. Goths, Vandals, Huns, and often Romans pillaged the cities, massacring the inhabitants or carting them off as slaves. A third of the people were slaves. Probably most Christians were slaves; remember, Christianity drew most of its converts from the poor and disadvantaged. The rich and educated clung to philosophy, paganism, and skepticism. It is interesting that it was the Gnostic Christians, drawn for the most part from the higher and better educated classes, who espoused reincarnation.

To most Christians the Church's offering of heaven or even purgatory must have seemed a blessed prospect. The last thing they looked forward to was coming back here. Nevertheless, the belief in reincarnation had many Christian followers. The subject was argued for more than 500 years before a Church Council finally decided to reject reincarnation as false.

The first great exponent of reincarnation was a priest named Origen who lived about A.D. 200. Students of church history consider him to be the most important philosopher and the greatest Bible scholar in the early Christian Church.

The authoritative work, *A History of the Christian Church,* by Williston Walker, has probably been used in more theological seminaries than any other book on the subject of the history of the church. It says of Origen: *No man of purer spirit or nobler aims ornaments the history of the ancient church,* and *Origen's theological structure is the greatest intellectual achievement of the ante-Nicene church.* Origen, Professor Walker says, gave Christianity a scientific standing, *an explana-*

tion . . . for him who would add to his faith knowledge.

Origen was hailed by the early Christian teachers who followed him as *the greatest teacher of the Church after the apostles* and *the prince of Christian learning.* The greatest philosopher of his time and one of the most famous thinkers of all time was Plotinus, who was not a Christian but a Neoplatonist. He and Origen had been fellow students of an unusual Alexandrian teacher, Ammonius Saccas. Porphyry, Plotinus' student and biographer, wrote that when Origen visited his class, Plotinus blushed and didn't want to speak on, saying: *"The zest dies down when the speaker feels that his hearers have nothing to learn from him."*

There can be no doubt that Origen was an extraordinary individual. A devout Christian, he wanted to die a martyr's death as a boy, when his father was martyred, but his mother convinced him that he should live to help her support the family. She hid his clothes so he couldn't run out and give himself up. By the time he was eighteen, he was so famous as a scholar that he was drawing large groups of students to his classes in Alexandria and later in Caesarea. To avoid slander from the close relations he had with them, he took Jesus literally and made himself a eunuch for the kingdom of heaven's sake. He was reputed to have written 6,000 books.

St. Jerome, who made the Latin Vulgate translation of the Bible, said it was impossible to read all of Origen's books, he wrote so many of them. Perhaps the greatest of his books was the Hexapla. In it he brought together in parallel columns the Hebrew Old Testament, a Greek transliteration of that work, and four Greek translations of it—the Aquila, Symmachus, Theodotion, and the Septuagint translations—with his own voluminous commentaries. Only fragments of this book, which would be of tremendous value to modern scholars, remain. Many of Origen's works have been lost. When, hundreds of years later, he was condemned by the Church as a heretic, most of his writing was destroyed or rewritten and scholars are agreed, he was often the victim of misquotation and unfair interpretation.

Undoubtedly, Origen had one of the most brilliant minds of his time. Perhaps too brilliant. His thinking was far in advance of his time. He was unable to accept many of the superstitions of his era and many of the inconsistencies he found in the early Church. He taught that many of the stories in the Bible were legend. That's a pretty standard belief of modern Bible scholars, but it wasn't then. He taught that the Bible should be interpreted allegorically, just as Unity has taught. He taught that the Jehovah of the Old Testament was too cruel a God to believe in literally. Origen couldn't believe in a God who would create human beings and then condemn them to eternal damnation. He taught universal salvation. He believed in the preexistence of souls, and he believed that we are given an opportunity to work out our spiritual evolution through rebirth and reincarnation. This powerful, compassionate, and brilliant thinker influenced every other Christian thinker for hundreds of years.

But in A.D. 553, both he and reincarnation were condemned by a Council called in Constantinople by the Emperor Justinian. Justinian is as interesting as Origen. As emperors go, he was one of the better ones. He began life as a peasant, but once he rose to the throne, he managed to restore the Roman Empire, which was falling apart, to some of its former glory. He won the city of Rome back from the barbarians; he reunited the eastern and western halves of the Empire; and—his greatest work—he unified all Roman law into one massive but orderly code, which has influenced our ideas of law ever since.

His empress, Theodora, was as interesting as he was. She'd been a prostitute and circus performer before Justinian made her Empress. Procopius, Justinian's official historian, left a secret book about them both. It was not a friendly book, but in it he says Theodora was so beautiful he wouldn't even try to describe her. She must have been. Justinian was mad about her. It would seem that she was just as capable as she was beautiful. The two of them felt that they not only had to set straight the affairs of this world but the affairs of the next world, too. They felt they were meant to be official arbiters of what Christian doctrine ought to be.

The work of Justinian's Council, in which reincarnation was condemned, is suspect. It was made up entirely of Eastern bishops subject to his will. The pope Vigilius refused to attend it, though he was Justinian's prisoner. The Emperor had kidnapped him and carried him off from Rome.

I doubt that Justinian called his Council

because he was particularly interested in condemning reincarnation. More likely, he was just trying to unify his Empire, and getting the Church to be a little more unified was a big part of his problem. There were so many different teachings, and some of them were extremely divisive. So Justinian gathered together such of the bishops as he had power over and put such pressure on them as he was able, to get them to anathematize some of the more divisive teachings in the hope it would help him to draw his Empire together and run it a little more smoothly.

The Council declared fifteen anathemas, condemning a number of teachings and a number of teachers. Actually, Origen and reincarnation were not specifically singled out, but the doctrine of the preexistence of souls was anathematized, and that was interpreted to include them.

Whatever Justinian had in mind, after the Fifth Ecumenical Council in 553, also called the Second Council of Constantinople, reincarnation was generally labeled as a heresy.

But don't think the belief in reincarnation then vanished. No, it persisted and grew. Remember, it was part of the basic religious belief of most of the people who lived in

Europe and Asia Minor, in fact, all of Asia. Not only the common people but the educated, the intellectuals, also believed in it. The Greek and Roman philosophers and thinkers—almost all of them believed in it.

Christianity was only one of the many religions in the Roman Empire, and various other mystical religions were powerful for a long time. Almost all of these believed in reincarnation. For a long time it wasn't certain that Christianity would become the dominant religion of the Empire.

A religion called Mithraism that had come out of Persia had spread all over the Empire. It was a soldier's religion. The soldiers loved it and carried it everywhere they went. Just a few years ago the ruins of a Mithraic temple were unearthed in London. Because the soldiers liked it, it had the support of the emperors, and for a long time it looked as if Mithraism might become the official religion of Rome. Had it become so, we would all be Mithraists, I suppose. It couldn't have won, however. Its victory was impossible. You know why? It had a fatal flaw. It didn't let women in. It was a man's religion.

But as I say, even though reincarnation had been declared a heresy, many people—

many Christians—continued to believe in it. By 1200, the belief had become so widespread, it almost overturned the Catholic Church.

Let's look at what the power of the Church consisted of, for it throws light on why the Church so fervently denounced reincarnation. The power of the Church consisted in its claim that it had power over your next life.

In the Bible, Jesus had said that He had power to forgive sins. Then in a very important passage—all important to the Roman Catholic Church—He passed this power to Peter. It's an interesting passage because in it Jesus is a bit of a spiritual punster. Peter's name in Greek is Petros, and the Greek word for rock is petra. Jesus says: *"I tell you, you are Peter* (Petros) *and on this rock* (petra) *I will build my church.... I will give you the keys of the kingdom of heaven, and whatever you bind on earth shall be bound in heaven, and whatever you loose on earth shall be loosed in heaven"* (Matt. 16:18, 19). The authenticity of this passage has been questioned by modern scholars, but it was generally accepted by the early Christians. Most of them believed Peter had founded the Roman Church.

You can see what tremendous power this gave the Roman Church. This is why the doctrine of the Apostolic Succession became so important to it. Jesus had the power to forgive sins, and He passed it on to Peter, and Peter passed it on to the popes, who had the power to pass it on to the priests who were loyal to them. Think how great this power was! You can see why the Church condemned the belief in reincarnation and established, as soon as it could, the doctrine that when you die you are transported immediately to heaven, to hell, or to purgatory. The Church held the keys to the next world. It had the power to secure you a cozy niche there—or send you to a hot one.

Belief in reincarnation does not rule out the power of priests and religious rites to lead you in a spiritual direction—these may have great power to keep you on a spiritual path—but it does place your fate mainly in your own hands. Your present life is what it is because your past lives have brought you up to here, and the nature of your future life depends on how you live this one. Belief in reincarnation strips a great deal of power away from the Church. You can understand why it wouldn't tolerate any such belief.

No, the Church and the priests who represented it held the keys to your next life—Jesus had passed to Peter, and Peter had passed to them, the power to forgive your sins and get you into heaven. Even if you were a terrible sinner, they could at least get you into purgatory.

Then the Church added a small refinement to this belief in its forgiving power. The Church taught that Jesus and the saints had been so good that they had more goodness than they needed to get into heaven, and they could bequeath this excess of goodness to others, who were sinners, who needed it. So in this way, there had accumulated what the Church called a Treasury of Merit, and the Church, as representative on earth of Jesus and the saints in heaven, could dispense this excess merit. Thus the Church became a kind of spiritual parole board and could shorten your sentence in purgatory. These shortened sentences—this time off in the next world—were called Indulgences.

The idea is not as strange as it may sound when you first encounter it. It is not hard to believe that someone very, very good—say, a saint, or an Apostle, or Mary—would have more influence in the next world than most of us. Mary or a saint might be a little more lenient, a little more forgiving, a little more understanding than Jesus or God! I feel sure there are more candles lit before Mary than anywhere else in a Catholic Church.

But with its great growth in power, the Church began to grow wealthy and corrupt. Priests began to sell Indulgences. This was part of what finally brought on the Protestant Reformation. But hundreds of years before Martin Luther nailed his ninety-five theses on the door of the castle church in Whittenburg, many people were beginning to question how spiritual the Church was. They wondered how such a material-minded organization could have any influence in the spiritual world. As a result of all this, many people lost faith that the Church and the priests had any power over their next life. The belief that they, as individuals, had to be responsible for their own next life, their own future existence, began to grow—and naturally, the belief in reincarnation began to grow with it.

The largest group that believed in reincarnation was called the Cathari. In France, they were called the Albigenses. In many parts of Europe, especially in southern France and northern Italy, the Cathari became so numerous they took possession of the churches and quit practicing Catholicism. There were so many of these Cathari that they threatened the existence of the Church. The Pope started a crusade against them. He got the kings and nobles to join him in attacking them by offering them the property of the Cathari if they destroyed them. Most of these Cathari were an unusually peaceful and gentle people; they were trying to live the spiritual life, and they had rejected the uses of this world. They believed the material world to be evil—look how material power had corrupted the Church— and they wanted to purify themselves from all materiality. That's where they took their name *Cathari*. *Catheros* is a Greek word meaning to purify. Reincarnation was their way to the spiritual purity they sought. Most of the people who have believed in reincarnation have believed in it for some such reason. The Cathari believed they had to be reborn until they had purged themselves from the taint of this material world, reborn and reborn again until they became pure spiritual beings, so that they could once more be one with God, as He had made them to be.

It took twenty years of fierce fighting to destroy the Cathari. Hundreds of thousands of them were slaughtered. It was a bloody crusade. The papal forces would sometimes go into a town and kill everybody in it. The story is told about a commander who attacked a little town in southern France, called Beziers. The commander asked the papal Legate, "Shall I let the Catholics off and not kill them?" "No," the Legate said, "the Cathari might claim they're Catholics. Kill them all. God will know His own." They killed 20,000 people in that one little town.

The Church's bloody extinction of the Cathari is inexcusable. But it was a cruel and bloody time, and reincarnation and the medieval Church were inevitably and unalterably opposed to one another. The power of the medieval Church rested largely on the belief that it could decide, or at least influence, your state in the next world. If reincarnation is true, no church or priest or anyone besides yourself has such power. So you can see why the Church leaders felt they had to do what they did. I'm sure they believed without question they were the divinely appointed defenders of the one true faith. Those who questioned the beliefs of the Church were enemies of God and the truth, bearers of false teachings that would lead people to hell, and it was an act of holiness to destroy them. The salvation of men's souls depended on the preservation of the Church and its beliefs, and the Cathari had become so numerous that the power of the Church hung in the balance. So out the Cathari had to go.

But even after they'd wiped out the powerful centers of the Cathari in France and Italy, the Church still couldn't get rid of the belief in reincarnation. Though the Reinaissance was a couple of centuries away, enlightenment was growing, and more and more people were beginning to think for themselves and to question the authority and teachings of the Church. All over Europe there were people who believed in reincarnation.

So the Church founded the Inquisition. The belief in reincarnation was the main reason why the Church founded the Inquisition. I never knew that until I began my research into this subject. But that's what brought this cruel institution into being—the Inquisition was founded mainly to rout out the belief in reincarnation. It shows how powerful the idea was and how widespread the belief in it must have been.

I'm sure the Inquisitors hauled down anyone who dared in any way to differ from the doctrines the Church had finally, after centuries of councils and much argument, decreed to be the true Christian doctrines; but the belief in reincarnation was the most dangerous to its power and authority, and it was this belief they pursued most relentlessly.

The Inquisition was brought into being to frighten people into orthodoxy. It tortured and killed hundreds of thousands, and put the fear of being pointed out as a heretic into everybody, so that there was little free thinking where it had power. Anybody could accuse you of being a heretic. You were not allowed to face your accuser or even to know who he was. If he won, he and the State got your property, which was not exactly an incentive to keep people from accusing you. Once accused, you were tortured to test whether or not you were guilty. For three hundred years the Inquisition went around Europe, frightening people.

Let me say here that the Catholic Church was not entirely responsible for the persistence and cruelty of the Inquisition. It had brought the Inquisition into existence because it felt its own existence threatened. But feudal authorities quickly saw its power as a means to amass riches and control unruly nobles who opposed them.

When we think of the Inquisition, most of us think of the Spanish Inquisition, which was by far the cruelest of them all. The Church was not responsible for this monster; the Church tried to prevent it and did what it could to restrain it. The Spanish Inquisition was instituted and carried out wholly by the Spanish monarchs, Ferdinand and Isabella, when they gained control of Spain in 1492. They used it as a means to destroy and to seize the wealth and possessions of those they considered their enemies, especially the old Moorish and Jewish families that had been at the center of Spanish life for centuries.

But in spite of all the Inquisitions, in spite of all the obstacles put in its way, the belief in reincarnation persisted and grew—and it's growing even faster today.

Once, after I made this lecture, a Catholic came up to me and said, "I wish you didn't have to be so hard on what we did to the Cathari—we're not that way now." I certainly agree with him; I have only friendly feelings for the Catholic Church as it is today. The medieval Catholic Church was the product of its time. It was no crueler than the Protestant churches were when they got power. The Protestants were just as quick to kill Catholics—or other Protestants who didn't agree with them.

People are still killing each other in the name of their religion, which is sad. But I sincerely believe there are more and more people in every faith who are willing to let other people practice their beliefs and their ways of life, however different they may seem.

Anyway, that tells the story of reincarnation and the Christian church.

So You've Come Up to Here

Christianity and the Church have never had many followers except in Europe and the Americas. What about the rest of the world? The facts there are clear and simple. The vast majority of human beings have always believed in reincarnation, the vast majority. The vast majority of human beings alive today believe in reincarnation. Part of the reason for this, of course, is that almost all of Asia believes in it, and the bulk of the world's population has always lived in Asia.

One interesting fact about human belief is that all primitive people believe we are immortal. Anthropologists have never found any tribe anywhere that doesn't believe human beings are immortal. I don't believe they've ever found any primitive tribe that doesn't believe in some form of reincarnation or transmigration. Primitive people believe that death isn't natural. You only die because somebody sticks a spear or arrow into you, or somebody practices witchcraft and kills you. Death is not natural. We are meant to live forever. That's what Charles Fillmore believed, too.

What about our world, the Western World, the Christian world today? It has been estimated, I don't know by whom, that ten to twenty percent of us in the Western World believe in reincarnation. That's in spite of fifteen hundred years of negative programming. You find, when you investigate, that this fifteen to twenty percent includes many of the most famous, the most intelligent people in history.

Intelligent people have always believed in reincarnation. The greatest thinkers of ancient Greece—Pythagoras, Plato, Socrates, Plotinus—all believed in it. Pagan Rome produced two great philosophers. One of them was a crippled slave, Epictetus; the other was an emperor, Marcus Aurelius. Neither of them wrote about reincarnation, but they both believed in it. We know they believed in reincarnation because they were both Stoics, and all Stoics believed in reincarnation—it was a tenet of their philosophy. Like the Cathari later, they taught that you are born again because you are a spiritual being and you have to purify yourself of materiality.

Throughout the Middle Ages, in spite of the persecution, there were always thinking people who believed in reincarnation. Giordani Bruno was burned at the stake because he believed in it. I don't see how a thinker, a philosopher, can help believing in it. David Hume, the great Scottish philosopher, declared: *Metempsychosis is the only system philosophy can hearken to.* Immanuel Kant and Kant's emperor, Frederick The Great—I don't know whether Kant convinced Frederick or Frederick convinced Kant—both believed in reincarnation. Hegel and Schopenhauer and Nietzsche and William James and Henri Bergson—they believed in it. A pretty illustrious list. Most of the great thinkers of the Western World, except those connected with the Church and those who don't believe in immortality at all, have believed in it.

Literature has as impressive a list. In Germany, you have Goethe and Schiller and Heine. In France, you have Balzac and Hugo and George Sand. In England, you have Blake and Wordsworth and Shelley and Tennyson and Browning. In this country you have Emerson and Thoreau and Poe and Whitman, and probably Mark Twain. Mark Twain had a strong mystical streak along with his humor. In music you have Wagner. In art you have Leonardo da Vinci. Benjamin Franklin believed in it. In our own age, you've had Luther Burbank and Thomas Edison and Henry Ford, and these are only a few.

Perhaps as interesting as any who have believed in reincarnation, because he was so explicit about his belief, was General George Patton. He hardly seems like someone who'd have such a belief, but he believed he'd always been a soldier, over and over. He'd been a defender of ancient Troy. He'd fought in Caesar's Tenth Legion. He'd been a knight in the Crusades. He'd fought for the Stuarts in Scotland. He'd been one of Napoleon's marshals. He even wrote a poem about it. I'll read it. Pretty interesting. It says:

> *So, as through a glass and darkly,*
> *The agelong strife I see,*
> *Where I fought in many guises,*
> *Many names, but always me.*
> *And I see not in my blindness*

What the objects were I wrought,
But as God rules o'er our bickering,
It was by His will I fought.
So forever in the future
Shall I battle as of yore,
Dying to be born a fighter,
But to die again once more.

Personally, I don't think I'd look forward to a life forever as a soldier. He would have been happy had he been a Viking. Maybe he was. In all fairness he must have been, because the Vikings believe—ah, like so many of the ancients, they have this very hazy notion about the afterlife. Dismal, oh, how dismal it was! You went to Niflheim, a world underground—a marsh, frozen marshes—the vaguest, most miserable sort of life. It was ruled by a goddess, whose name is very familiar to us, Hel. Ah, yes, Hel was a woman.

But not everyone had to go to Niflheim. If you died in battle, it made a difference—the Valkyrie came and picked you up, put you back together if you had been dismembered, and transported you to Valhalla, Odin's Hall, and there you spent the night feasting and getting drunk; then the next day you marched out on the battlefield and fought all day; then after the battle the Valkyrie came again, picked up all your pieces, put you together, again took you back to Valhalla, and you spent the night feasting and drinking again, getting ready for the morrow's fight. Patton would have loved it, wouldn't he?

But Patton truly believed in reincarnation. He told how when he took over his first command, he was sent to France, to a little town called Langres, and a young French officer offered to show him around the town, and he said, "You don't have to. I know this place." He said, "I told the driver where to go, almost as if someone were at my ear, whispering the directions. And I took him to what had been the Roman amphitheater, the drill ground, the Forum, the Temples of Mars and Apollo. Some of these were torn down, but I had been there before." Patton had no doubts about reincarnation.

Have you ever had an experience like this? It's called deja vu—already seen. Most people, I'd say, have had them. I've had a number of such experiences. One thing certain about them—when you have one, it is as vivid and real as any you will ever have.

Several years ago my wife and I were driving up the West Coast on California Highway #1, and we decided to drive out to Point Reyes. You drive for miles across rolling meadows that fall down to the sea. This was a different kind of country than any I had ever been in. Perhaps it took me by surprise because we'd been driving for days through precipitous views of the sea, redwood forests, and eucalyptus groves. But as we drove down the curling road, a sense began to build in me that this country, so unlike any I'd ever seen, completely strange, was not strange at all. It was a familiar country, a country I knew intimately. It's hard to tell you the feelings that stirred in me. They were excited feelings, feelings of anticipation, feelings that I was returning to something I cherished and loved, and hadn't seen for a long time, elated feelings, feelings I was coming home.

Yet at the same time I knew it was not this particular spot, not Point Reyes. No, it was just that this spot—its features so unlike any I had ever, within my memory, experienced— had brought into my mind a vivid awareness of a place just like it, a place I had no memories of, but I knew well. I'm not a geologist, so I don't know what you call this kind of landscape, but I know that somewhere on

earth, near some other seacoast than California's, there are just such undulating hills and
hollows rolling down to the sea. Once I
roamed there and I know that place and remember it—though perhaps remember isn't
the right word—with love.

Let me describe one more such experience,
not exactly the same but similar. This is a recurring fantasy, but much more vivid than
any fantasy or dream. It doesn't come at will
or at any certain time or place. But I'll close
my eyes and suddenly I'll be walking—or perhaps it's more accurate to say I'm being
transported, because it doesn't seem to take
any effort of my own—swiftly, silently, along
a road that runs along the top of a range of
high hills, from whence I always seem to have
an unobstructed view of the river that runs
far below me. The hills on both sides of the
river are high; I might better call them moun-
tains. The river is broad, strong, and I sense,
deep, though I've never swum in it. I think
it's a tidal river, a mighty tongue of the sea.
The sea, I know, is not far away, though I've
never gone there. I feel this might be a fjord,
but I've never seen a fjord and there's no precipitous rift of rock.

But more impressive than the wide river

and the high hills is the dense forest that descends in a green tide from the hilltops to the water's edge and rises green on the farther side to the green crest of the hills again, stretching green as far as I can see up and down the river from horizon to horizon.

When in my mind I have been carried there, I've always had a sense of a place I know and love—revisited. Whatever I may have been doing or thinking, for a long time after I've returned, I've been at peace.

Interestingly, I wrote the description of this place several years ago for one of my books. Since then, much as I'd like to, I've never been able to find my way there again.

As I tell these stories, I realize how probably I'm failing to get across to you the sensations, the feelings, the sense of reality that is mine. As I've said about all such subjective experiences, when you try to tell it to someone else, it all somehow gets milked down and you can't convey it.

But to get to the essence of my belief about reincarnation, this is what I believe: I believe I am making an immortal journey, and I've come up to here. That's all. I think that's all we need to say. I'm making an immortal journey. I've come up to here.

I love that phrase, "I've come up to here," because I think it describes the human condition. Here we are. Here and now is what we've come up to on this journey. I got the phrase from a Hopi Indian. It's a Hopi phrase. I got it in a way that utterly convinces me there's a lot more to the world than seems to be here.

I used to be responsible for teaching all Unity ministers, and I'd have special classes for them that weren't just religious; I believe ministers should know a lot about a lot of things. One time, in one of these classes, we were reading a biology book, "Man's Emerging Mind," by a biologist named N. J. Berrill. It is a beautifully written book, full of stimulating ideas. In the middle of this book, he mentions the Hopi Indians, and he says in effect that in their language they have no way of putting an idea in the past or future. In English we do this by conjugating a verb. We put an "ed" on it and that puts it in the past, and we put a *shall* or *will* in front of it and that puts it in the future. When I read this I thought, "Gee, what would that do to you, if you had no tenses?" We are all prisoners of our language. You think the way you think to a great extent because you think in English and English has a certain structure, and if it had a different structure, the way you think would be different. If I had no way of making an easy past and easy future, what would that do to my thinking?

So I sent one of my students to the Kansas City Public Library to bring back what he could about the Hopis. Well, all he could find were a couple of books that showed little hogans on the mesas and a few Indians sitting in front of them. But, about two weeks later the tour guide at Unity Village called me on the phone and she said, "Jim, there's a couple down in the Silent Unity Visitors' Chapel who would like to meet you. Could you come down?" So I went down and she introduced me to Chief Frederick Whitebear of the Hopi Indians, and his wife, Naomi.

What are the chances, just because you'd like to know something about the Hopis, of a Hopi chief walking into your office? It must be at least millions to one. You can say, "Oh, well, just a lucky coincidence." But as I said about my mother's telephone call when I was grievously in need, I don't believe in lucky coincidences or unlucky ones, either.

As it turned out, Whitebear is probably the leading authority on the Hopis. He told me a number of things about them. Berrill, by the way, was not exactly right about their language. Among other things, Whitebear said, "Often when two Hopis meet, they will say to one another, 'Ah, so you've come up to here.' " I thought, "Gee, isn't that a great phrase, because it's so true of us. It's a perfect description of the human condition. We've come up to here."

Chief Whitebear had come to see me because he'd had to come to a town in Kansas. An anthropologist was writing a book, "The Book of the Hopi," and Chief Whitebear was his consultant. He's listed on the title page. It seems that he and his wife had liked my writing through the years, so they decided, "Let's go over to Unity Village and see if we can meet this man Freeman." So, in walked the Hopi chief. You may not believe this, but I believe that it was because I had sent out a call, and after meeting Whitebear and reading "The Book of the Hopi," I can see if someone were going to respond to a mental call like mine, a Hopi Indian would be a likely responder. They are very unusual people with a long, long history of dedication and practice of spiritual principles. There is no question in my mind that Whitebear heard me and came.

The world is not what the world seems. Surely you realize that. You and I are living in the midst of a mystery, and it's great. It's not a mystery because it doesn't have meaning—it's a mystery because it has so much meaning we can't grasp it. We haven't come up yet to the place where we can do that— we've only come up to here.

Life has set me down in the midst of a mystery

It seems beyond my fathoming . . .

Yet this much I see clearly—the mystery is not mystery because it is meaningless but because it is meaningful. It is not because things have so little meaning, but because they mean so much that I cannot grasp the meaning.

How shall an inchworm comprehend a continent?

But let the inchworm measure the mystery of a leaf or two, and it may turn into a butterfly and master even the mystery of air.

And if an inchworm can turn into a butterfly, who shall say what a butterfly may become?

I am God's inchworm and God's butterfly.

106

O God, I inch my mind across the mystery that is my world, measuring it as best I may. Sometimes, if only for a moment, I encounter a meaning that is like light and an assurance that is like love.

Then, though I cannot see the meaning clear, I know that whatever the meaning is, it is not less but more. And whatever I am, I am more, too.

And whatever you are, you are more, too.

I believe I've lived in many worlds and many times and many places. I wrote a poem about this once. I'll read it to you. During these talks I'm going to read some of my writing. Actually, I just read you a piece of it, only I didn't tell you it was my writing. It's from my book *Prayer: the Master Key.* I like my writing, and I hope you do. As I told you at the beginning, I've written many pieces that relate to this subject, and I think they say what I want to say as beautifully, as movingly, as clearly as I can say it. So from time to time, I'm going to read some of them.

I wrote this poem for *Daily Word. Daily Word* gives me a picture, and then I've got to write something to go with it. I've written about four hundred poems this way. In this case, it was a photo of a boy looking out over a hill. I'd had a phrase in my mind for a long, long time—"a wind from far away, out of forever"—but I hadn't been able to write a poem to go with it.

Now I wrote the poem:

A wind from far away out of forever
Blows sometimes from I know not what
strange strand;
Then I am as in a dream, a dream I never
Remember, yet somehow I understand.
I turn, although I know no road
returning
To the high country whence my mind's
winds come
To fill me full of dreams and full of
yearning.
What fair land, what far shore the wind
blows from,
I cannot say, but when the wind is
blowing
It blows to me a sense of truths more
true,
Of lives beyond this life, and worlds past
knowing.
Companions, does the wind not blow for
you?

It's hard for me to believe that such a wind hasn't blown for all of us at times. The world is infinitely more than we think it to be, and if we get to thinking we know all the answers, it's only because we haven't asked enough questions. The world is stranger, lovelier, more meaningful than any meaning or loveliness we can find in it. And so are we.

Some Different Views

Among the ancients there are two famous thinkers who rejected reincarnation. Lucretius, in his long, long poem, *De Rerum Natura,* (Of the Nature of Things), argues that it's ridiculous to think that the soul, if it survived death, wouldn't remember its former life. He writes:

Why can we not remember something, then,
Of life-time spent before? Why keep we not
Some footprints of the things we did of old?

His purpose was not so much to dispute reincarnation as to prove that the soul has no existence independent of the body, and he uses our inability to remember any other existence as part of his proof.

Lucretius believed we are physical beings

bound by physical laws, and when physical activity ends, the life of the mind or soul ends, too. There is no reincarnation, there is no immortality of any kind. There is no soul to survive. When you're dead, you're dead.

Aristotle also did not believe in reincarnation. His disbelief was especially important. The theology of the Catholic Church has been deeply influenced by his philosophy. Aristotle's thinking has had an influence on all our thinking ever since he thought, even when he was wrong.

Unlike Lucretius, he didn't hold that physical life is the only life. He didn't deny the reality of God or soul. In fact, it was his ideas on the nature of soul that caused him to reject reincarnation. He wrote an essay about soul, *De Anima* (On the Soul).

Just what Aristotle believed about the soul is not easy to determine. Aristotle isn't an easy writer to understand. He's had hundreds, probably thousands of interpreters, and they don't agree as to what he says. He deals with abstractions in an extremely abstract way, and his writing about the soul is especially abstract. As far as I can see, he believed the soul is tied to the body and could have no existence separate from it. Let me give you a few quotations from his *De Anima*, and let you decide what he is saying.

The soul, he says, *is "the essential what-ness" of a body.* The soul is *a substance in the sense of the form* of the body and thus, it is the *actuality of the body.*

To ask whether soul and body are one, he says, *is as meaningless as to ask whether the wax and the shape given to it by the stamp are one. . . . It indubitably follows that the soul is inseparable from its body, or at any rate that some of its parts are.*

Aristotle's soul has three parts. There is a nutritive soul, whose business it is to keep us alive and provide for our physical needs. There is a sensitive soul, by means of which we contact and react to the world around us. And there is finally the rational soul, by which we apprehend truth.

This rational element in soul he also calls "mind." Mind, he says, is not bound to the body and cannot be destroyed. However, only a few creatures have mind. I believe Aristotle equated mind with the power to think logical-ly and abstractly, as did he.

At any rate, as a result of all this logical analysis and rational abstraction, Aristotle decides that when we die, our nutritive and sensitive souls can no longer exist, for they no longer have a body to exist in or any senses to sense with.

This leaves only our rational soul or mind. Since it deals only with pure thought, it is not bound to materiality, so it survives. But the consideration of timeless truth is its only function. So after death, all that continues to exist of us is our rational soul, contemplating its own impersonal rationality. All in us that moves, all in us that senses, all in us that feels—that hopes and fears and desires—all in us that makes life what it is and makes us what we are ceases to be. Existence continues, but in a kind of metaphysical oblivion. There would be no memory, because our rational soul would not be concerned with the personal contacts, reactions, and events we remember.

Actually, if you compare Aristotle's rational soul to the Hindu *purusa* and *atman* or the Buddha's *anatta*, no-self, that nevertheless acts like self—all of which I will discuss at greater length in a few minutes—it's hard not to feel they are all much alike. I suppose you can show by careful analysis that they're all quite different, but when I think what it would be like to be any of them on a day-today basis, I have a strong sense of six of one and half a dozen of the others.

The new metaphysical religions, like Unity, teach that we are Spirit, soul, and body. Spirit is the animating, vitalizing spark that is God in us. This is what Unity calls the Christ self in us, the perfect and eternal being that God made us to be when He made us in His image and likeness. Soul is that part of our being that makes each of us what we individually are. In its deepest elements, the soul is one with Spirit and is fed by the ever-renewing springs that flow from the world-ground of being, and at its surface it becomes our mind and sense organs that enable us to perceive and experience the world at the level we have come up to, to communicate with other forms of life, and to be what we seem to be. Soul contains conscious and unconscious elements. You might think of soul as a kind of computer tape, if you can conceive of a computer tape that is composed of a spiritual substance, one that is alive and intelligent, self-programming and self-editing. Body is the outpicturing in physical manifestation of the inner pattern of our soul. However, when we have perfected ourselves, body and soul will be integrated with Spirit. In truth, we're spiritual beings living in a spiritual world. Again, when we try to describe what we really are, we don't seem far from Aristotle or the Hindus.

I'm sure a philosopher or theologian can show there are great metaphysical and theological differences between all these concepts. Charles Fillmore made much of the difference between intellectual understanding and spiritual understanding. The East has a different notion of what truth is than the West does; at least East and West seem to be seeking it in different directions. This doesn't surprise me. I believe all great truths, including the truth about truth, are paradoxical.

When Pilate asked Jesus, "What is truth?" there's no record of any answer. I've always liked that. It would indicate that truth may be beyond anything we say it is. If Pilate had asked that question of Einstein, Einstein would have said, $e=mc^2$. If he'd asked the Buddha, the Buddha might have said, "I haven't elucidated that. Just follow my path and you'll stumble over it." Or he might have begun to chuckle, as he and his fellow *arahats* sometimes did when they'd been discussing the transcendental nature of things. They felt that truth is that *wherefrom words turn back, together with mind, not having attained.*

The Greek philosophers like Aristotle arrived at truth through words and mind, that is, through logical thought. They invented the syllogism, with its major and minor premises and conclusion, as in the famous example familiar to most school children, "All men are mortal. Socrates is a man. Therefore Socrates is mortal."

We in the West want a truth we can put into words or mathematical symbols and arrange in a logical pattern. These words and symbols—we call them scientific theorems and laws of nature—spell out our knowledge about the world. They've given us great power over it, to manipulate it and change it.

The Hindu philosophers like Sankhara or the Buddha are just as subtle and just as adept at abstract reasoning as the Greeks, but the truth they are seeking is more an intuitive one. The Eastern thinker seeks not so much to hold truth in his mind as an idea he can analyze and handle. Instead he wants to identify with the object of his thought. Perhaps we should say that he does not so much want to know the truth *about* something as he wants to know the truth *of* something. Words about truth are not enough. He does not feel he has the truth of anything until the nature of that which he is trying to know the truth of enters into his nature.

A modern philosopher named F.S.C. Northrop has analyzed the two ways of thought in a book called "The Meeting of East and West." He says that the basic world-ground of being—the basic reality—of nature and of our nature—is an undifferentiated, indeterminate continuum.

I am sorry to have to use such polysyllabled phrases, but when you deal with philosophers and especially metaphysicians, you are likely to encounter them. For myself I have found it worthwhile to struggle with the way they say things, for sometimes these men are probing deeply and effectively into the nature of things and sometimes, by seeking to understand what they mean, I have come on wonderful insights into truth. So I hope you will think about this "undifferentiated indeterminate continuum." Perhaps what such a phrase is saying is that the ultimate reality is beyond our power to describe in such terms as we have to describe it in. But Northrop says that there are two ways of approaching it and giving it form. One is to approach it aesthetically and empirically—that is, to sense it, to feel it, to incorporate it into yourself, or even better to immerse yourself in it; actually to become it. The other way is to approach it theoretically and rationally—that is, to think about it, to turn it into logical statements and mathematical equations, that mind can grasp and master.

In *Prayer: the Master Key,* I have tried to show the difference with an example.

The Easterner, wanting to know the truth of bamboo, goes and sits in the bamboo grove. There he listens; there he watches; there he lives. He puts down roots with the bamboo; he puts forth stems and leaves; he himself grows one with the earth and opens his heart to sun and rain. Until at last he cries out, "I am bamboo!"

The Westerner, wanting to know the truth of bamboo, consults a book about it. He sets up tables and mechanisms to analyze its growth and content. He records its history from seed to fodder. He sections and blueprints it. He learns everything there is to learn about it. Until he can say, "Bamboo is any of various woody or treelike grasses of the genus Bambusa or other related genera, as Arundinaria, Dendrocalamas."

In the West, the fact finder reduces things

to thoughts.

In the East, the thinker becomes the thing.

Perhaps I can show the difference simply. You can know all the facts about a chair—its dimensions, its structure, its materials; or, you can sit in it.

But I wonder if the difference may not consist more in philosophic conjecture about the difference than in actual practice, in real life. In real life, I think we think both ways without thinking about which way we're thinking.

What Are We?

Before we can go any further in our discussion of reincarnation, we have to consider one fundamental question: What are we?

What are we? If we are to believe in reincarnation, or for that matter if we are to believe in heaven and hell, or in any kind of survival after death, this becomes the first and most fundamental question we have to consider—if we survive after death, what is it that survives?

Throughout the rest of these lectures, this will be the most important—and probably most difficult—question we have to consider. What am I? What are you? What is it that reincarnates?

For the most part we just accept the fact

that we are. We are aware of our existence. That is enough. We don't ask what we are. We are—why, we are, uhhh—this obvious fellow you are looking at and talking to. But who or what is this obvious fellow? How obvious is he?

Oh, I am aware of my personal limitations. My inadequacies are plain enough. If I look without, I come quickly to my fingertips, my toenails, my hair. If I look within, I come quickly to the end of my knowledge.

But how much more am I than this physical body—this "me" that eye can see and ear can hear and hands can touch—which seems to be me! When someone warns you, "You kick me when you kick my dog," you may learn with a bloody nose that this is literally true.

Tear down some country's flag—a mere bit of colored cloth—on a tiny island in the Pacific, and you may touch a patriot five thousand miles away to the quick, so that he rushes forth to kill or be killed to avenge the insult you have inflicted on him.

As bigots and oppressors have many times found out, you may pile blazing fagots flaming hotly around the martyr's limbs, and while the fire consumes his very flesh, he may serenely sing dear hymns of faith.

Is this obvious fellow then—this conscious self I am usually so conscious of—what I really am? Is this my true self? Or is this simply part of me, one aspect of me, as my hand is part of me, or my heart, or the invisible wisdom that takes care of the manufacture of red blood cells in my bone marrow, or that in me which flashes ideas into my conscious mind for it to form into a poem?

We are not as easy to lay hold of as we sometimes seem. The truth is that we are not thought, not body, not passion, not feeling, not appetite, not emotion, not will, not conscious mind, not subconscious mind, not any of these things, nor all of them, but more. We are not to be explained in psychological, economic, social, political, biological, or religious terms. All of these explain aspects of our nature, but aspects only. Separately and altogether, they are not enough. We are yet more.

What are we then? As I say, I will return to this subject in a number of these lectures, but as a starting place, let's go to India.

I'm no Hindu. I'm too much of a Westerner. The West is my world. It's where I live and it's the way I think. I reject what it seems to me is the basic thesis of Hinduism, which is that we live this life best when we live it learning to reject all that this life counts as important—except spiritual growth. While I value spiritual growth, I do not think that the barefoot monk sitting in silent meditation is the supreme embodiment of human achievement.

Personally I have never been able to accept the notion of withdrawal, detachment, separation that dominates Eastern thinking. In the Five Great Vows of the Jains—Jainism is a Hindu religion—you see this view of things carried to its ultimate. Let me give you just one of these vows, the fifth: *I renounce all attachments, whether to little or much, small or great, living or lifeless things.* What this vow implies is spelled out by the Jains in considerable detail; it means that we should form no attachment to anything we see, anything we hear, anything we experience with any of our senses; nothing our senses disclose to us should be of any importance to us. That is about as conclusive and universal a rejection of life and the world in which we live as one can conceive. True, not many Hindus live by such a vow, but the ideal is there.

The East believes we have to be reborn—it believes this more universally, more fervently than any other part of the world. But the purpose of all this being reborn is so that at last we can avoid being reborn, so that we can be released from the strain and pain of birth, death, and rebirth, released from the misery this world brings.

Some of my friends tell me I'm unfair to the East. Perhaps I am. But it seems to me its basic view of the world is that it's such an unpleasant place, the only reasonable attitude one can take toward it is, it's something one wants to get out of. Something in my Western—American?—nature rejects this view of the world. I'm too much a child of the West.

The Hindus, the Jains, the Buddhists sometimes describe the world—and us, too, as physical beings in the world—almost in terms of loathing. The first great truth of the Buddha on which he bases his whole system, is: life is suffering. Certainly any intelligent human being has to agree that life has suffering in it; no one escapes it. But to say that life *is* suffering, as the Buddha says, is to take an entirely different view of it.

The world is the world I've come up to, that's all. I wrote a piece once where I asked God why He hadn't made a perfect world of bliss.

One day when I was talking with God, I said to Him, "Dear God, why did You make the world as You made it? You are perfect Intelligence and perfect Love. Why did You make the world the way it is instead of the way it might have been?"

So God said to me, "Look."

Then I had a vision of the world as perfect. I looked and saw it radiant and complete.

The perfect galaxies circled in perfect glory through perfect absolutes of emptiness.

The perfect sun shone in the perfect sky. The perfect birds soared in the perfect air. The perfect lamb played with the perfect lion. The perfect trees gave of their perfect fruit. And in all the perfect cities there was only the perfect activity of perfect beings.

I saw infinity immaculate and orderly, perfect beyond all praising, and I saw it consummately full of perfect things.

Then I saw that I was running. As hard as I could run, I ran around and around that perfect world. But nowhere in all its glittering perfection could I find what I was searching for.

At last I could not bear to search any longer. I fell down and hid my eyes in my hands, and I cried out, "But dear God, where am I?"

Again God said, "Look."

I looked and I was in my own room. Around me were my soiled, familiar daily things—the ruffled carpet, the scarred desk, the papers not too neatly sorted out. Through the window where the curtain hung somewhat awry I could see the bare branches of the tree blowing in the sometime wind.

"But God," I said, "this is my usual world."

"It is the world," said God, "as I have made it to make you in it. Tell me, please, what world is better than that?"

Can you think of one?

Let me read yet another passage from another of my books. I've written a great deal about the meaning of things, and when you talk about the meaning of death and dying and life after death, as I am in these lectures, the meaning of things is what you are talking about.

This is from my book, *The Case for Believing.*

This is a world that fits me perfectly and a world into which I fit perfectly. It is no better and no worse than I am, and I am no better and no worse than it is. We befit one another;

we deserve one another; we complement one another.

Am I not a chancy, changing thing and is it not a chancy, changing world?

It is a pleasant world and I love pleasure.

It is a world that brings pain and I am not hard to hurt.

It is a world full of things to desire and I am a creature full of desires.

It is a world of many mysteries and I am a creature of much ignorance—but with a hunger to know.

It is a world that sometimes gives and sometimes withholds and I am such a one who may perhaps love one or two and give myself to something more than myself.

It is a world that can be turned into a hell or into paradise, and I can turn it into either one.

It is a world of day and night and ebb and flow, a sometime world as I am a sometime being.

It is a world where things grow old and die because they have not learned how to live and stay alive—and is this not the case with me? But it is a world where nothing perishes though all things change, and I feel sure this is my nature, too.

It is a world where I can grow to be more

than I am.

But above all, it is a world where I can be me while I am growing . . . .

This is, I think, the perfect world for me. I don't like to think this because it has so many imperfections in it. But a world that has me at its center—and here I am—will have good and evil, pleasure and pain, beauty and ugliness, love and selfishness, life and death in it until I have grown to be more than I have yet become.

Many people of the East have apparently agreed with me, they don't like the idea of withdrawal either. For the teaching that swept Asia and won millions of followers was not a religion of withdrawal. It is Buddhism, but not the Buddhism of the Buddha. The Buddha himself, as I say, taught a very stark religion. Life is suffering, and our one aim is to attain nirvana. What nirvana is, the Buddha never said; but its meaning comes from the image of a flame. The word means literally "blown out," and a reasonable definition is extinction, at least from life as we know it.

But there is a much modified form of Buddhism called the Mahayana. Buddhists liken their teaching to a ferryboat that will transport us from the sufferings of this world to the bliss of the other shore, that is, to nirvana. Mahayana means big ferryboat in contrast to the Hinayana, or little ferryboat that is the religion that has stayed closer to the original teachings. Mahayana Buddhism is the religion that swept Asia. It is not the religion of the Buddha, but the religion of the Bodhisattvas. When I think of the Bodhisattvas, I think how much like Christ the idea of the Bodhisattva is.

Bodhisattva is a beautiful word—it has been translated as "Wisdom Heart." The aim of the Bodhisattvas is not nirvana; it is to remain in this world and help others to escape from suffering. The great Bodhisattvas take vows that they themselves will never enter nirvana as long as one human soul—nay, one solitary creature, even the least—remains outside the gate. This means, as you can see, that they will always remain in the world, because there will always be some creature that needs their help.

Anyone can be a Bodhisattva. A Bodhisattva is anyone who decides he will devote his energies henceforth to becoming a Buddha, that is, an enlightened one, a Savior, anyone who sets out on the path of spiritual unfoldment.

There is a great Mahayana teaching with which I can fully agree. It goes like this: samsara is nirvana.

Samsara and nirvana are Sanskrit words. Sanskrit is the ancient language of India. Samsara is the round—the round of birth, death, and rebirth—this life. Nirvana, as I have said, is indefinable. But it implies a state of spiritual perfection in which we are freed from having to live this life, freed from the painful round of birth, death, and rebirth.

What are we saying, then, when we say Samsara is nirvana? Aren't we saying that it is right here and now that we must find fulfillment? Aren't we affirming that if we put off our fulfillment until we arrive at some perfect state of bliss like nirvana or heaven, we will put it off forever? We must find fulfillment now, doing what we are doing, being what we are being, whatever pain and imperfection we may find ourselves in.

Only when caterpillars are caterpillars will butterflies be butterflies. So, when I am a caterpillar, let me be the best caterpillar I am capable of being; then some day I may be a butterfly. I've often wondered if the caterpillar knows that. Surely somewhere, deep down in its unconscious nature, a caterpillar senses its ultimate wings—and the butterfly, in some part of its being, does it not retain the image of the caterpillar?

We have to find our meaning living this usual life. If we keep seeking it somewhere else, it will always elude us. One of the great Zen masters is asked, "What is satori?" (another word for nirvana). He answers, "Walk on." If we try to put this in our own Western terms, we might say something like: We have to live here and now. Earth is also heaven.

Many years ago I wrote a little piece of verse as I walked across the fields of Unity Village. When I wrote it, I had no thought about samsara or nirvana. I'm not sure I'd ever heard of either of them. I was just walking on, thinking what I was thinking, feeling what I was feeling, being what I was being. But today, as I was thinking about this Eastern truth, samsara is nirvana, I suddenly realized that my little poem expresses it beautifully. That's the great luck of being a poet. You walk about listening for the truth and sometimes you hit the mark without taking aim. This is the verse. It was called, "Had We the Eyes":

How fair a world around us lies,

Heaven unfurled, had we the eyes
To see the worth of all that is;
Like heaven earth is also His.
How can the rose, more than the clod
From which it grows, embody God.

Isn't this what Jesus is telling us when he says, "The kingdom of heaven is within you" or as other versions of the Bible put it, "The kingdom of heaven is in the midst of you"? The kingdom of heaven is among the heaven-hearted, wherever they are, and that is the only place it will ever be.

We're here to build the new Jerusalem. Not somewhere else. Not later. Not in some different mode of manifestation. Not on some different level of existence. We're here to bring forth God's perfection now. I believe this. I believe I am here to transform the world into a better place to live. You can't work all your life as I have, in a great prayer ministry like Silent Unity where your whole reason for being is to help people who need help, without believing this and doing all you can to bring it about. My great prayer has been, "Lord, help me to help people to be what they are meant to be."

Today more and more people are becoming interested in spiritual matters, and they are discovering that the great religions of the East contain great spiritual truths. But most of us don't believe, as the East does, that our supreme goal is to dissolve into nirvana. In spite of what some religions teach, most of us have very little faith that our goal is to die and go to heaven.

We want religion to teach us the nature of spiritual laws and principles. But people today are science-minded. Science has taught us about physical laws, but then it has shown us how to work with them to improve our health, to prolong our life, and to make a better world for all of us to live in. We believe religion should do the same from a spiritual standpoint.

That is why religions like Unity are having a powerful influence. They deal with spiritual laws and principles, but then, like science, they show us how to use them to make a better world. Thus, Unity is a mysticism, but it is a practical mysticism. It acknowledges the truths of every religion, but it stays in the mainstream of Western—that is, American— thought. As I've already said, Unity is not only an American religion; it is Americanism in religion.

But let me return to the subject I was starting to discuss before I let myself be carried away with the thought that East is East and West is West, and never the twain shall meet, which, as I have just admitted, I find after further reflection is not entirely true, for they do meet in such insights as samsara is nirvana and the kingdom of heaven is within you.

I was saying, if we want to know more about reincarnation and about our own nature, we can turn to no better source than the teachings of the Hindus.

Thus, the Hindus surround the self with physical-psycho-spiritual sheaths, each one coarser and grosser as it moves from inner to outer manifestation, with the sense-body—the one we think of as body—as the outermost, and the spiritual being—the Hindu word for it is atman—as the inner and only reality.

Many ancient myths of many ancient people surround the naked soul with seven veils, much as the Hindus do. The Babylonian goddess, Ishtar, the embodiment of the life principle, must let these veils fall from her before she can enter the land of the dead to find her lover, and she must clothe herself in them again before she can win her way back and bear Tammuz back to the world of the living. Aphrodite, too, must strip to her nakedness when she seeks to bring back Adonis.

In our time we tend to mock at myths, but scholars are beginning to see that myths are no less carriers of truth than scientific equations are. When you find a myth that is told in different languages by different people, you have not come on a foolish fable. More likely, you have come on something we human beings feel to be true in deep, instinctual levels of our being, but we lack the abstract terms in which to express it. Perhaps there are none—this is a different kind of truth—and so we wrap it in a story.

I believe the Hindus know a great deal about the physiological psychological composition of us human beings. They know this because, for thousands of years, they've put their very best minds to studying it. When Nehru was prime minister, one of the members of his Cabinet resigned so that he could go into the jungle and meditate on his own nature. The Minister of Commerce, I believe it was. And their brightest people have been doing this throughout their whole history— for at least four thousand years.

For the last four hundred years, we of the

West have put our best minds to studying the external universe. The very best minds we've had have been out there trying to figure out what the material world is like—and they've created marvels, haven't they? Just think, electric lights and power, flight to the moon, computers, atomic bombs—you cannot name all the things, they have changed our world so much. Just four hundred years of our best minds.

The Hindus for four thousand years have put their best minds to sitting still, gazing at their navel, and asking, "What's going on inside me? What am I?" Well, if we could do the things we have done in four hundred years, you may be sure they have done some marvelous things in four thousand. They are just as bright as we are. Every bit as bright. But they have put their psychological-physiological discoveries in Eastern terms—in their own terms—so they talk about auras and *prana* and *bodhi* and *kundalini,* about astral bodies, and all that sort of thing.

But this is not our language, the language of Western science, and many of us have come to believe that for something to be accepted as a fact, it has to be discovered by scientists and put in scientific terms. So we brush off the East's four thousand years of study, almost without looking at it, as being without substance. "Occult!" we say as if that dismisses it. But occult merely means hidden, covered up—and what knowledge is not, at least until we explore it and try to uncover what is covered up and find out what it is that is hidden?

Finally, after four centuries of studying the nature of the external world, we of the West are seriously beginning to study our own nature. Psychology is the newest science. When we know as much about ourselves as the Hindu sages do, who have for forty centuries been studying their psychological-physiological nature, though not in psychological-physiological terms, I believe we will find out that they knew a great deal about what we are. But we will put our knowledge in psychological-physiological terms, and then we will accept it. We'll say to one another, and probably to them, "Look at the great new scientific truths and facts of nature we have discovered." And we'll come up with scientific instruments like biofeedback machines.

Every culture has to express its truths in its own terms. If you try to express truth in terms of another culture, it will not work. That is why Christianity has never been able to convert Asia.

However, as to why Christianity has not converted Asia, I like the remark made by a famous missionary of the last century, the Abbe du Bois. He said Christianity might have had a chance to convert India if it had not been taken there by Christians.

On the other side of the coin, however, the various Hindu and Buddhist gurus who are now plying their Eastern faiths in this country will find they never convert more than a fringe few people here. We are all children of our own culture, our own world.

Every hospital can happily have a biofeedback machine. If you'd go into a hospital and talk about yoga and auras, they would laugh you out the hospital door. But biofeedback, that is scientific.

Until auras and the like are put into scientific terms, we are not going to accept such foreign-sounding items, however true they may turn out to be.

It is interesting that artists have always adorned saints with a halo, or depicted them as glowing. Is this merely an artistic convention to indicate holiness—or is it that we do glow, and the glow shines more clearly through the spiritually-minded, and artists, more skilled at seeing what most of us do not see, feel this glow and try to depict it?

Several years ago a scientist at Yale (I've forgotten his name) conducted experiments that showed that each of us is surrounded by an electric field of force. I don't know exactly what his experiments were and I don't know if much has been done to follow up his findings, but that is not important in relation to what I am saying here. What I am saying is that this is the route we have to take, the route of scientific experiment with findings we can express in scientific terms, if we expect to find acceptance and credence. We refuse to accept an aura, but a field of force, ah, that is scientific. We learned about fields of force in our high school physics class. It's as easy to believe in a field of force as it is hard to believe in an aura.

Personally I like the idea of having an electrical body that is a field of force, or if that sounds too Hinduish to you, a field of force around my body. It offers a possible explanation for something I have always wondered at. In my body are hundreds of different kinds of cells—almost unimaginably different—as different as the thin elongated neurons that run from my brain clear down to my toes, and the little round platelets that revolve in my blood. I am hundreds of different kinds of cells. But in my beginning just two cells fused together and made one cell in the womb of my mother. Only one cell. But this one-cell-me formed cells in all these hundreds of different forms, and I turned out normal—at least I think I am—just the right quantity of each kind in just the right places. How did I do that?

If I'm a field of force, that offers a possible explanation. In that one first cell that I was, there was at its center an arrangement of chromosomes. Ever since then that same arrangement of chromosomes has been at the center of every cell I've had, no matter how different in shape those cells may appear to be. If an electrical field of force emanates from that central chromosomal arrangement, such a field may be an invisible pattern that determines what every cell will be and where it will be placed. This would explain how I managed to grow to be the complex arrangement of complex cells I've become. Yes, I can believe I do have an aura—oops, pardon me, I mean a field of force. If spirit or soul has a physical carrier, surely it's this chromosomal spiral that appears in the one cell we originally were. This arrangement of genes that appeared when we were conceived and has been at the center of our every cell since, this—on the physical level—is our true shape, our true image.

One thing about the East's teaching as to what you are, all the religions and philosophies of the East believe you are a spiritual being, living in a spiritual world, governed by spiritual laws, and you are on the path of spiritual evolution. Your goal is to know your spiritual nature.

I am not going to make a thorough study of Eastern thought as to what you are. That would take many hours.

There are a number of schools of Eastern thought. Since I have mentioned the Jains, it is only fair for me to describe their belief.

Jainism is, as I have said, an absolute denial of the value of the things of this life. It is an illuminating commentary on the mysterious way the world is made that the Jains are among the richest people of India. The gods, I have always maintained, have a sense of humor. Their ancient Law of the Opposites is one way they have of expressing it. It contains a warning—let us not hold forth too long and rigidly in an extreme position, lest we discover to our discomfiture that we have arrived at the opposite extreme.

The Jains imagine the world to have the shape of a gigantic man—or woman. Do not think that this is such a strange belief as it first sounds. Genesis declares that Jehovah made man in His image and likeness, which would certainly indicate that the primitive Jews thought that God is a man, and He must have been thought of as a universal and gigantic one. Emanuel Swedenborg, the brilliant Swedish scientist and Christian mystic, envisioned heaven as a man—and wrote of "the grand Man, who is heaven." He likewise envisioned God as a man. Anthropomorphism has not been an unusual human belief. To the Jains the world is a gigantic man, and you as a living entity exist as a separate soul-fleck of being within this universal figure. If you are material minded, you may exist at a level no higher than the feet. As you deny materiality, you rise to higher levels. The goal is to rise to the topmost point, the crown of the head of this world-being. They call this state *kaivalya*. You do this by eliminating your karma, which weighs you down. I will discuss karma at greater length in a later chapter.

Most of us live at about waist level. Below are those whose bad karma has plunged them into one of a number of hells. Above are those who are purifying themselves of the burden of karma.

You have to get rid of your good karma as well as your bad karma. Good karma is even harder to eliminate than bad karma. Bad karma clings to us painfully, but we may cling to good karma, because it brings us pleasant experiences; it may even enable us to be as gods.

The goal is to eliminate all karma, every shred of it, so that we may rise into the crown of being, the highest level, where we float isolated and serene, nothing remaining of us but the self-luminous bubble of spirit, not unlike, when you think of it, Aristotle's third part of the soul. Also when you think about it, you can see that it is not unlike the view of heaven some Christians have, where the archangels soar forever singing around the throne of the Eternal—except that in the Christian view we think of the singing angels as a choir, while the Jains think of them—each one—as a solitary and silent being. The word philosophers usually use to describe such a unit is *monad*.

Jainism is not the most widely influential of the religions of India, but it is not atypical. It is very ancient. Scholars believe it originated with the Dravidians, who had an advanced civilization in India when the Aryans invaded around 2000 B.C. Modern Hinduism—Brahmanism—seems to be a mixture of Dravidian and Aryan teachings. Probably if you probe deeply in any of the schools of Eastern thought, you find that, though names and details may differ, in their essence and in the effect they have on their devotees' way of life, they are all much alike.

The East has a great teaching: Truth is one, many are its names. Or they may say, God is one, many are his/her names. Unlike the West the East has not been reluctant to imagine God in female form.

The Hindu teaching we are most likely to be familiar with is the Vedanta. Vedanta is a Sanskrit word that means the end of the Vedas. The Vedas are the Hindu scriptures. The Vedanta teaches monism, that is, everything is one. There is only Brahma—God if you prefer the word—and God is all. Your goal is to realize your personal non-reality and your oneness with the One. It sounds not unlike Christian Science, doesn't it?

You as a separate, distinct personality and your world of thoughts and things—*nama-rupa*, names and forms the Hindus call it—are appearances, the illusions of maya. *Maya* is the word Hindus usually use when they refer to the world of appearances. We often translate the word *maya* as meaning illusion. The dictionary says it is "the sense-world of manifold phenomena used in Vedanta to conceal the unity of absolute being." It is Brahma—basic reality—as it appears to be as you experience it from the aspect of the many instead of the One.

Maya is an interesting word. It is more familiar to us than we think, though not exactly in that form. Sanskrit, the ancient Hindu language, is akin to English. Maya is related to the very first words most of us ever spoke—ma, mother. Maya to the Hindus is the mother principle. Ma, maya, what a fertile word! We get words like magic and might and majesty from it, and the merry month of May, when the life-power restores our world in spring. Maya is the force that produces the many-splendored world of appearances, "all the ten thousand things," and it is also the world of appearances that is produced.

Then there is the teaching called Sankhya. This is the teaching usually associated with yoga. The Sankhya is a dualism. The world that in the Vedanta is maya, illusion, merely an aspect of Brahma, in the Sankhya is real. It is called *prakriti,* the Hindu word for matter, but your mind as well as your body is *prakriti.* In all the Hindu schools, our mental processes as much as our physical processes are considered part of the material world. The Sankhya teaches that *prakriti,* which includes your body and mind, is real, but it is not you. You are *purusa,* pure, transcendent spirit, the true self, and your goal is to realize that you have no part in, you are no part of, *prakriti,* the world of mind and body, thoughts and things. You are *purusa,* separate and perfect, flawless and complete.

Then there is the teaching of the Buddha. The Buddha, Gautama Siddartha, was a Hindu, and his teaching is not too unlike the Vedanta or the Sankhya, except that he taught there are two unpleasant truths that lie at the root of existence. It's because these are basic to the nature of the world and of us that we have to suffer. One he called *anicca,* nothing permanent. There is nothing permanent. The other he called *anatta*, no self. There is no self, no *atman*. You can see that these are tremendous negatives to build a teaching on. Nothing permanent. No self.

"Of permanent fixed being I see no sign," he said. The ultimate reality out of which the entire phenomenal universe has been brought forth, he called *sunyata*, the void. Everything, all of us—in our ultimate essence, we are emptiness, nothing.

As is the case with the Jains' belief that the world is a gigantic man, this belief should not sound too strange to many ears. The strict Catholic doctrine teaches that God created the world ex nihilo, that is, out of nothing.

Some have interpreted the Buddha's teaching to mean he didn't believe in God. Personally, I don't think he was denying that there is an underlying reality, what Tillich has called the world-ground. He never said what nirvana was like, or told what the conditions would be when, using the ferryboat of his teaching, you left the miseries of this world and arrived on the other shore. Sometimes when he and his students who had reached enlightenment with him were discussing the Transcendental Wisdom of the Other Shore—as they called it—they would just quietly begin to chuckle. But whether he believed in God or not, the Buddhists have plenty of gods; they even made a god of the Buddha.

I'm not a Buddhist, but I think he was a brilliant thinker, and I love the way he refused to think of himself or his world as fixed entities. He saw his world and he saw himself as process. I think it's important that we look at things this way. If we think of ourselves and our world as fixed entities, that is the way we're likely to remain; we are likely to stay fixed.

The world is alive; it is changing and growing. You are alive; you are changing and growing. This is just the you and the world you've come up to at this moment. How important it is never to lose sight of this truth. "You cannot drink out of the same stream twice," the Buddha said. Tomorrow you will be more—or less.

With his belief that there is no self, you may ask how the Buddha could believe in reincarnation. What is there to reincarnate? But the Buddha believed in reincarnation as much as anyone; it is fundamental to his teaching. True, you don't have an eternal self, as it was in the beginning, is now, and ever will be. But you are composed of constantly changing states of being which he called *skandhas*. These are your power to form a body, your feeling nature, your reason, your sensing and knowing faculties, and your instincts and subconscious nature. At death these separate, but they are elements in the flux of being, and just as they were drawn together to form you now, they will be drawn by the force of their own motion and by the force of the flux of being in which they move, to form you again. There is a famous selection from Buddhist scripture called, "The Questions of King Milinda" that takes up this problem.

Said the king (King Milinda): "Bhante Nagasena, does rebirth take place without anything transmigrating?"

"Yes, your majesty, rebirth takes place without anything transmigrating."

"How, Bhante Nagasena, does rebirth take place without anything transmigrating? Give an illustration."

"Suppose, your majesty, a man were to light a light from another light; pray, would the one light have passed over to the other light?"

"Nay, verily, Bhante."

"In exactly the same way, your majesty, does rebirth take place without anything transmigrating."

"Give another illustration."

"Do you remember, your majesty, having learnt, when you were a boy, some verse or other from your professor of poetry?"

"Yes, Bhante."

"Pray, your majesty, did the verse pass over (transmigrate) to you from your teacher?"

"Nay, verily, Bhante."

"In exactly the same way, your majesty, does rebirth take place without anything transmigrating."

"You are an able man, Bhante Nagasena."

If you think about the Buddha's teaching and that of the more orthodox Hindus (remember, the Buddha was born a Hindu prince) in the light of their implications, you see that however different they may seem at first, they end up with the same results. Whether you think of yourself as a permanent entity or as a changing process, you reincarnate and reincarnate until you achieve the ultimate goal of being. However different the abstract reasoning may be, though the Buddhist goes out one door of the mind and the Hindu goes out the opposite door, by the Law of the Opposites they meet on the road to the same goal, whether they call it *moksha* or *turiya* or nirvana, or whatever, the state of merging their identity in what F.S.C. Northrop has called "the undifferentiated, indeterminate aesthetic continuum," out of which all things emerge and into which all are submerged again.

The Buddha's ideas bring to mind the thoughts of Christian mystics like Meister Eckehart, who said, "God is nothing," by which he meant God is no thing. And is this not true?

Perhaps we should take a few minutes to discuss the teachings of the mystics, for the mystics, although they describe reality as indescribable, have a great deal to say about what we are and what the world is.

Most of us, when we think of mysticism, think of something mysterious, strange, occultish. That is because the word in common usage has acquired a second meaning, and when we say of some belief, "It's a mysticism," we usually mean it is something spooky and insubstantial, without sound basis. But mysticism, as it appears in religion and philosophy, is not a vague and insubstantial belief. It is a very ancient type of philosophy and perhaps has had more adherents than any other approach to life.

It flourished in Egypt, Greece, and Rome from the sixth century before Christ. Pythagoras, often thought of as the father of philosophy, was a mystic. Plato was profoundly influenced by mysticism. Plotinus was a mystic. Mysticism pervades the writing of St. Paul. The Gospel of John is a mystical work. St. Francis was a mystic. A long line of mystics, like Eckehart, have influenced all Christian thought. A number of denominations, like the Quakers and Anabaptists, are mystical. Al Ghazzali, the most important Moslem theologian, was a mystic. So were Zoroaster, the Buddha, Confucius, Lao-tzu, Moses, and Mahomet. Mysticism is the dominant philosophy of India and China.

The dictionary defines mysticism as *the belief that direct knowledge of God, spiritual truth, or ultimate reality can be attained through subjective experience (as intuition or insight).*

That is not a bad definition, but it leaves out certain essential elements of mysticism.

The mystic believes that you can know and experience reality, but you cannot adequately describe it. It is from this belief that mysticism derives its name. Reality is beyond grasping with your mind or putting into words. Nothing you can say about it suffices. The names that can be given are not the absolute name.

But though you cannot describe reality, the mystic believes that you can have a direct encounter with it. For in and through and under all that is, within and beyond all the evanescent phenomena constantly appearing and fading away on the surface of this swarming world, there is an underlying universal, enduring reality, a world-ground, an undifferentiated, indeterminate continuum, a central truth of being. You may call it what you will. Most of us simply say, "God!"

You can experience this central truth of being, and when you do, you discover that it is the central truth of your own being. The indescribable universal reality, that is the essence of all that is, is one with the equally indescribable reality that is your true self. You are one with the One.

There is a beautiful expression of the basic truths of mysticism in the Chandogya Upanishad. The Upanishads are part of the Hindu scriptures. They are prose discourses, originally delivered orally to students sitting at the feet of Hindu sages (Upanishad means "sitting near devotedly") who lived more than 2,500 years ago.

A boy Svetaketu, asks his father to explain what is his true nature and the true nature of the world. The father says:

"Fetch me from thence a fruit of the Nyagrodha (fig) tree."

"Here is one, Sir."

"Break it."

"It is broken, Sir."

"What do you see there?"

"These seeds, almost infinitesimal."

"Break one of them."

"It is broken, Sir."

"What do you see there?"

"Not anything, Sir."

"My son, the subtle essence which you do not perceive there, of that very essence which you do not perceive there, of that very essence this great Nyagrodha tree exists. Believe it, my son. That which is the subtle essence, in it all that exists has its self. It is the True. It is the Self, and thou, O Svetaketu, art it" (Sacred Books of the East, edited by F. Maxmüller; Vol. VI).

In another story, which I have adapted, the

boy asks, *"Please, Sir, inform me still more."*

The father says: *"If someone strikes this great tree at its root, it bleeds, but it lives; if he strikes it in the middle, it bleeds, but it lives; if he strikes it at the top, it bleeds, but it lives; it stands firm and luxuriant, pervaded through and through by the living Self, drinking in its nourishment. But if the living Self leaves one of its boughs, that bough withers . . . and if it leaves the whole tree, the whole tree withers.*

"In exactly the same manner, my son, know this: This body withers and dies when the living Self leaves it, but the living Self does not die.

"That which is the subtle essence—all that exists has its existence in that. That is the True. That is the Self. Svetaketu, that art thou."

The father gives a number of similar illustrations, ending each one with the words, "That art thou," or "Thou art it."

You can almost sum up what mystics believe about world-reality and your individual reality in two Hindu phrases: *Neti, neti,* not this, not that, and *Tat twam asi,* That art thou. The real is not anything you can point to or describe. Anything you say it is, it is not that. Yet when you penetrate clear to the ultimate reality of being and experience it, you realize that it is the ultimate reality of your own being. That art thou.

Mystics may describe their indescribable encounter with reality in many different ways, depending on their era, culture, and religion. They may say they had a vision, or they saw God, or they talked with an angel, or they entered nirvana or samadhi, or they simply caught a glimpse of the Truth.

The one thing they have all reported is that although the truth they find, the reality they experience, is beyond their power to report in words, it is good. The central reality of being is good beyond all concept of good, unutterably beautiful, inexpressibly beneficent, so good that it leaves them ecstatically enthusiastic about the ultimate meaning and purpose of life.

No one has the mystic's experience and remains unchanged. From then on they become people of insurpassable peace and unassailable love. The apostate becomes the apostle, the wastrel becomes the saint, the peasant becomes the poet, the ordinary man or woman becomes the maker of the river crossing, the gateway to truth for thousands of other human beings.

It is hard to discount their experience as illusory and merely subjective, for not only do they themselves come out of the experience profoundly changed, they have profoundly changed the world for all of us. They have founded most of the world's religions.

As we consider the works and lives of mystics, it is hard not to believe that there is an illumining, life-altering encounter with reality open to human beings that mere intellectual effort cannot achieve, but which can only be gained by a sincere and persistent discipline of the soul, by giving one's self to something higher than one's self. This experience of truth is so different that we cannot describe it, but we can assimilate it and be assimilated by it, after which we live, as it were, in another dimension of being, one in which the things of this world are of small consequence, one of such unshakable peace, power, and love that it cannot even be comprehended by those who have not attained it.

The Hindus tell some wonderful stories about what you are, stories that illustrate the fact that as long as you are in this world of *nama-rupa*, things and thought, as long as you remain under the magic spell of maya, the law is change. Hundreds of these stories have accumulated through thousands of years. They are beautiful fables, and they make a powerful point. Many scholars believe that Aesop's fables had their true origin in India. Let me tell you one of these old folktales.

The story is about a man named Narada, a Hindu sage who lived long ago. Narada sought with all his heart to learn the hidden truths of being, and as a consequence of his ceaseless meditation and austere, saintly life, he became such an illumined soul that he grew very close to Vishnu, one of the greatest of Hindu gods. The two had many conversations about spiritual matters.

One of the things Narada wondered about most was the mystery of maya: how did it bring about its magic transformations so that one passes from life to life, always different, yet always the same? So one day as he and Vishnu sat meditating in a secluded grove beside a quiet pool, Narada said to Vishnu, "Lord, I would like to know the secret of your maya. Can you reveal that to me?"

The god said, "No one has ever comprehended the mystery of maya. It is not wise to seek its secret."

But Narada insisted, and finally the god said, "Very well. Come with me."

The two arose and together passed out of the peaceful grove.

It was a very hot day. The sun blazed down on them as they walked across the bare, dry land. After they had walked awhile, Vishnu turned to Narada, and said, "My son, I am thirsty. Over there in the distance, shining under this merciless sun, I see the roofs of a little village. Will you go there and fetch me a pitcher of water?"

"I will go at once, Lord," Narada said, and he set off across the fields toward the cluster of houses while the god relaxed under a little hillock.

When Narada reached the village, he stopped at the first house he came to and knocked at the door. The door was opened by a beautiful girl who looked at him with warm, soft eyes and a gentle, welcoming smile. The sage, whose life had been spent in isolated self-denial and meditation, had never before felt so close to anyone so warm, inviting, and beautiful as he felt now. As he gazed into her eyes, he felt drawn as by a vision. When he asked her if he could have a drink of water, she gladly let him into the house. Once inside, his only thought was for the beautiful woman whose delicate hands held out to him his drink of water.

Narada completely forgot that he had come to obtain a pitcher of water to carry to the god. He forgot the god. All that day he thought of nothing but the girl. The day passed. The family seemed glad to have such a saintly man staying with them, and were delighted that he showed such interest in their daughter. They made him feel unreservedly welcome. They invited him to their table. They pointed out a bed where he could sleep. Narada stayed day after day.

After a suitable time he asked her father if he could marry her. They were married. Narada became a member of the family and entered into the life of the householder. Twelve years passed. They had three children. When his father-in-law died, he became the head of the family, and lived happy and content with his wife, his children, his fields, and his cattle.

But in the twelfth year, the rainy season was an unusual one. Violent storm followed violent storm. The river began to rise. Finally one dark night, a fierce thunderstorm burst upon the village. The river rushed over its banks and the little village was deluged. Houses were carried away, men and animals had to swim for their lives. Narada placed his smallest child on his shoulders, with one hand he led the two bigger children, with his other hand he clasped his wife, and the little family set forth through the flood. But he had not gone far before he stumbled in the raging torrent that tore at his feet, and the child was thrown from his shoulders. When he reached out to recover him, the two other children were swept away, and though he clung to his beloved wife with all his strength, the rolling waters quickly tore her from his side. Head over heels, grasping and choking, Narada was whirled away by the dark flood until at last he was tossed unconscious on a little hillock. When he came to, he found himself surrounded by a muddy sea. Desolate, he began to weep disconsolately.

Suddenly behind him he heard a gentle voice. "My child, you went to fetch a drink of water for me. I have been waiting for you. You have been gone for almost half an hour."

Narada rose and turned around. Where there had been raging water, there was now only the bare, dry land baking in the blazing sun.

The god was standing beside him, an inexplicable smile on his lips, the same inexplicable expression in his eyes. "Now do you comprehend the mystery and power of maya?" he asked.

Personally, I don't believe, as the Buddha did, that there is no self. I believe there is. A few times in my life, I feel I've caught a glimpse of this self.

There is that which we see when we look from face to face. But there is also that which we can see when we look from spirit to spirit. But because it's so easy to look from eye to eye, we've programmed ourselves to experience each other just as forms and faces and voices and such. And that suffices us. But a few times in my life—they were very anguished moments when I had to look beyond face and form, and even mind—I had to look with eyes of love. Ah, yes, we have to look with eyes of love when we want to look that deep, that close, that far. But a few times when I have looked with eyes of love, I think I've seen the real self of another human being. I can't describe what I saw. All I can say is, it was a vision of inexpressible beauty. That's all. I believe that is what I'd see if I saw the real self of you, and that is what you'd see if you saw to the I of me. A vision of inexpressible beauty!

In Unity we refer to the real of us as the Christ self, and we say, we are made in the image and likeness of God. The image and likeness of God—that would be inexpressible beauty, wouldn't it?

But when we talk about an eternal self, it makes us sound like an everlasting entity, something finished, something fixed, that has always been and has never changed.

I don't like the feeling that gives me. I have a deeply intuitive feeling—whatever I am, I am not fixed. At my essence, I'm alive, I'm growing. Life is alive, and what made me is Life. As I've said, I've always like the Buddhist notion of self as process. But I also believe I have a real self.

How do I reconcile these two ideas: eternal self, perfect and complete, and continuous process, always changing and unfolding?

In one of my books I've tried to do this. I like the Hindu thought that "words turn back, together with mind, not having attained." When you try to describe the indescribable, you have to resort to poetry.

I had been writing an essay trying to answer the question: What is the I of me? and I had been struggling to bring my abstractions together.

I had asked, Am I most like a diamond, come perfect from the hand of my Creator, unaltered, immaculate, as I was in the beginning, am now, and always will be, the same perfect diamond? Or am I most like a river? A river is change. It changes no matter how you look at it. Walk along it, and it changes with every step. Stand still, and it changes with every moment. Then into my head flew one of those inspirations only poets sometimes have. I've written what these feel like, too. I've said, "Angels sing in me. I rush to write down what I hear." This is what my angel said about the self:

What am I then?

Conceive if you can something that is like a diamond—shining, flawless, always the same—and just as much like a river—changing, flowing, never the same—and you have caught a sense of the I of me.

Perhaps I am most like a song.

What is a song?

A song is a thought in the imagination of its composer, an unheard music of the mind. A song is words and notes set down on a sheet of music paper. A song is a sweet undulation of sound for a little time in a certain place. And a song is also the singer singing—a mind and body expressing themselves. I am the song and the sound and the singer.

You will hear me again and again, in different keys, in different voices, whistled and chanted and hummed, sometimes only a few bars, sometimes sung over and over. The singer may sing imperfectly, yet I am always the same perfect song, imagined music in the mind of my Composer, written down in the Eternal's musicbook, flawless and complete.

I am His song. Listen for me.

You are His song. Listen.

Karma or Free?

As I have said, if there is a God, He must be just. That is the least we can imagine Him to be. We cannot conceive of such a creative power as God as being unjust. If God is just, then the world He creates must be just. There must be an explanation for the seeming injustices, especially the inequities of birth. I see no way we can view this life as the work of a just God unless we view it from a larger frame of reference than this single life.

You can't read one page and know what a book is like, or hear one chord and know what a piece of music is like. Likewise, to give this life meaning, you need to see it as one in a series of lives, with lives leading up to this one and lives ensuing from it.

166

Imagine waking up one morning and seeing a friend dragged out into the town square and shot. Then see another friend being led forth at the same time and awarded a medal. If that were all we knew, we'd think, "What a horrible world!" But if we knew that yesterday one friend had murdered his neighbor and the other had risked his life to save his neighbor, we might think, "That explains what happened to them."

In real life we see such seeming inequities many times. One person has a pleasant life; another an agonizing one. One is born a prince; another a beggar. The prince may be a brute and a fool, and the beggar may be a scholar and a gentleman. The accidents of life load one—undeserving as far as you can see— with every kind of blessing and reward; the accidents of life pile misery after misery—undeserved as far as you can see—on another. Hamlet in his "to be or not to be" soliloquy lists some of life's injustices, and asks:

> *"Who would bear the whips and scorns*
> *of time,*
> *The oppressor's wrong, the proud*
> *man's contumely,*
> *The pangs of dispriz'd love, the law's*
> *delay,*

The insolence of office, and the spurns
That patient merit of the unworthy
　　　takes . . .
Who would such fardels bear,
To grunt and sweat under a weary life,
But that the dread of something after
　　　death,
The undiscover'd country from whose
　　　bourn
No traveler returns, puzzles the will?"

We would add, do not these same "fardels" puzzle the intelligence as well? For who, seeing such inequities and injustices, could possibly convince himself, if he has any power of reason, that this life is aught but a meaningless accident—unless there is not only a life beyond this life, but also before this life we lived lives that brought us to the time and place and circumstances we find ourselves in here? And yes, to the particular personality we happen to be wearing in this act of the play. *Persona*, remember, was the Latin name for the masks all actors wore on the ancient stage.

As I have said, to believe that life makes sense, you've got to believe two things:

One, we are immortal.

Two, we draw our own life to us.

We've discussed the first, immortality. Now, let's consider the second. Do we draw our own life to us, and if we do, how do we do it?

Some of us blame our lives on God. We say, "God willed it," especially if it's something unpleasant.

Well, perhaps God does will it. But God has to have, among other qualities, intelligence. In fact, traditional theology defines God as the rational principle in the universe. There's no way that intelligence—the divine reason—would will what is unreasonable and unjust. Reason would will that you should have what you rightly and reasonably draw to yourself.

Probably, if you ask most people who believe in reincarnation how we draw our life to us, they'll say, "Through karma." You can't investigate reincarnation without coming on the word *karma*.

It's a Sanskrit word. It simply means deed, work, action. It comes from a Hindu verb that means "to make." That's what karma is to those who believe in it. It is that which makes us what we are and makes our life what it is.

I don't like to use the word *karma* any more than I like the word *reincarnation*. It's a good word, but it's a dangerous word, because when we talk about karma, the word carries such negative implication. Karma lies over the East like a cloud. The East speaks of good as well as bad karma, but it's all bad, because it all binds you to the wheel of birth, death, and rebirth. Good karma may be worse for you than bad karma because you don't want to let it go.

When we in the West interpret the word, we usually say it means the law of cause and effect. We think that makes it all clear, because it sounds scientific—the world is run by the law of cause and effect, isn't it? I don't like the law of cause and effect either, because I don't like determinism. If there's anything I don't believe in, it is predetermined lives.

The doctrine of predestination—the doctrine that by divine decree souls are born to be saved or lost—is the worst sin Christian theologians have inflicted on our world.

The belief in predestination lies like a burden on Islam, too. Moslems call it kismet, fate. Among both Christians and Moslems, the belief arises out of the sincere desire of the devout to glorify the greatness of God: God is supreme; therefore, His will must be the determining factor in everything that happens. But this presents a dilemma. You do as you will, but it is really God's will that guides you. God has decided at your birth how your life will turn out, though you are responsible for the decisions you have to make.

God guides you into good actions, yes, but God leads you as He will. That's why we have the phrase, "Lead us not into temptation," in the Lord's Prayer. This may not be what Jesus said. The phrase may be a mistranslation. It came to be generally accepted because it is in the King James Bible, the only Bible we had until recent times. The King James Bible was translated from the Vulgate, which was a Latin translation from the Greek Septuagint, which was in turn a translation of the language in which Jesus spoke the words. Latin lacked the aorist of the imperative passive form of the verb, which was the form used in the Greek Septuagint, so it could not reproduce the exact meaning of the words. English also has no such form.

Ferrar Fenton in his translation of the Bible says it should be: *"You would not lead us into temptation."* There are two great translations from the Aramaic, the language Jesus used. George Lamsa in his translation says: *"Do not let us enter into temptation,"* and Charles Cutler Torrey translates it as: "*Let us not yield to temptation.*" Unity, which does not believe in predestination, says: "*Leave us not in temptation.*"

However, the idea of predestination has long been firmly fixed in religion. The Moslems express it in their great prayer, the *Fatiyah:*

> *Guide us to the straight path,*
> *The path of those whom You have*
> *favored,*
> *Not of those who have incurred Your*
> *wrath,*
> *Nor of those who have gone astray.*

Paul expresses the idea even more bluntly in Romans, where he says that God will have mercy on whom He will have mercy, and He will harden the heart of whomever He will. God is the potter, and He can make any kind of clay pot He decides to make. What right have clay pots to complain? Apparently Paul thought of living souls as clay pots. Augustine for the Catholics and Calvin for the Protestants hardened Paul's statement into an official creed.

I have a different view of God and of human souls. God is great, but He is not a dictator. It is not because they feel powerful that dictators keep their people in bonds. On the contrary, it is because they do not trust in their own authority. A truly powerful government sets people free. I do not believe that it is different with God.

God is the Creative Principle of being, and He would not make anything except to live creatively. God is great enough that He does not have to ordain our lives to prove His greatness. In all the universe, look where I will, I see nothing fixed and finished. God does not make us fixed. He makes us free.

There is a magnificent passage in Dostoyevski's "Brothers Karamazov," where one of the brothers enumerates some of the dreadful things he has seen happen to seemingly innocent people in this world and cries out that if God has built His heaven on the blood of one innocent person, He can take His ticket back.

That's the way I have always felt about a God-foreordained world. I have said this many times, and now I say again: "I am free. This I believe with all my heart. If there is any meaning and if there is any dignity and if there is any importance to anything that is, I am free. If I am not free, then all that seems to have meaning and dignity and importance becomes only the rattle of machinery—even if the machine be God's!

"All the brave acts of heroes and all the selfless acts of saints—even the cross—become merely the motions of puppets in a puppet show. Though the whole world be the tent and God Himself the Puppeteer, it is still only a puppet show—hardly worth the price of admission."

There is something in every human being that tells him he is free. We realize how much we are creatures of habit, but still there is something in us that says, "I am free."

I don't like theories, theological or scientific, that make us feel predetermined. Predestination and the law of cause and effect can turn us into machines if we let them. I am not a machine, and I refuse to let anybody make me into one.

I've always liked the Chinese idea that everything in the world is made up of two interacting energy modes called the yin and the yang. Everything is what it is due to the interplay of these two fundamental forces: the yang, active and positive—and masculine; the yin, passive and negative—and feminine. You know a man originated the concept. The yin and the yang are never thought of as fixed and stationary. They are moving and alive, always in dynamic action. One is constantly becoming the other. A brilliant Chinese insight puts at the very center of yin a touch of yang, and at the center of yang a touch of yin. That thwarts a deterministic view of the nature of things. There's an unaccounted-for, unpredictable element in everything that happens. That's a beautiful thought!

Another reason I don't like the word *karma* is that too much of the time karma becomes a judgment, whether you call it a law or call it God. Most people who talk about karma think of it as something that is going to see we get punished for our sins. I don't believe in a God or a karma that punishes me. I wrote a piece about this.

There is no sign in nature of a principle that punishes. There is only the sign of a healing power, a righting power. When I break a law, I suffer the consequences, but the law does not punish me. It merely acts to restore the balance. That is all the law is trying to do—to restore the balance, to set things in harmony again. If I eat the wrong food, which I sometimes do, my stomach does not curse me or judge me; its concern is not to punish me. Its

*sole concern is to handle the unwise food as
wisely as it can—to set things right for me. If
I cut my finger, my finger does not upbraid
me or punish me for my wrongdoing. It just
sets out immediately to heal the wound. Is
God inferior to my finger or my stomach? I do
not believe it. The universe does not want
pain. It wants growth. It is never interested
in punishing me. It is interested in my well-
being, for my well-being is the well-being of
the universe.*

As much as anyone, the apostle Paul has
probably been responsible for giving us this
notion of a mean God. He not only said that
God can make us into bad pots, if He wants
to, in Galatians he says: *Do not be deceived;
God is not mocked, for whatever a man sows,
that he will also reap.* (Gal. 6:7) Most of us
have quoted this, or had it quoted at us, and
we listen to it as if it were the absolute truth.
By gum, you're going to reap what you sow!
Like the law of cause and effect, like karma,
the law of sowing and reaping lies over us like
a big cloud.

When I was a little boy—and probably
most of you are like me—God was a big
bearded figure, sitting up in the sky, hiding
behind a dark cloud, peeking out at me, and

He had a big book, and He was writing down all my sins and mistakes—that's why He had such a big book. A few years ago I wrote an essay about sowing and reaping, about God as the judge. It's called, "The Seed and the Harvest." It's in one of my books, *Of Time and Eternity*.

I'm a gardener, and I make a point in my essay that is a gardener's point. This law of sowing and reaping, of karmic fixedness, is at best a half-truth, because I've never reaped anything I sowed. I go out in the early spring and sow some little brown pellets about the size of beebees. Now the last thing I want back is a little brown pellet. What I reap are not little brown pellets, but things many times larger and much more savory. What I reap are radishes, round, red, juicy, and crisp. If I reaped what I sowed—little brown pellets—I'd be very unhappy. I don't. I've never in my life reaped what I sowed. I've always reaped something much more wonderful than anything I've ever sown. Well, not always. Because this isn't a precise world, in spite of karma and the law of cause and effect. It's a very imprecise world. Do you know what I often reap? If you're a gardener, you know. Weeds. Right, weeds. Or we may even get something altogether unexpected, as people sometimes have. Suddenly a new variety appears—a new apple, or a new rose—all sorts of things, and we have something different from anything we have ever sown.

Also, I reap where others sow. Thank God for that! How miserable this life would be if we didn't.

Charles and Myrtle Fillmore sowed Unity. I'm so glad. Some unknown somebody sowed buttons and buttonholes. Isn't that great? What if we had to think up everything ourselves—like the wheel and jet planes and scissors and printing? I rejoice as I reap all sorts of things I never sowed.

Sometimes God sows! I don't believe God predestines our lives, but sometimes, when we give Him an opening, God steps in. Then life really changes. I've had that experience, too.

No, the law of karma, the law of cause and effect, the law of sowing and reaping, is not a universal truth.

Stop and think about the world. The sun does not act the way it acts because it hopes to reap what it sows. The sun sows its light because it is its nature to sow the light. It gives what it has to give. That's all. That is what everything in the world does. That is what we ought to do.

I wrote a piece about this. I'm going to read it because it's beautiful. It's the end of the article I told you about, "The Seed and the Harvest." In it I say:

To give, to give as fully and freely as we can, not so that we will be blessed, but so that life will be blessed, should this not be our highest aim? Does not the universe set this example? Nothing in it reaps what it sows. Everything gives what it has to give. The universe does not say, "Dance, and you must pay the piper," but "Dance the dance you have in you to dance." You only pay the piper when you dance his dance, not yours. And the universe dances to no dismal one-note tune. Its music is a medley of melodies, different, but in harmony, where even the dissonances, if they are your note, merge into the magnificat of life.

There is a law of sowing and reaping, but it lies on the world not like a judgment, but a promise. It is the law of creativity. And it says, "Sow and you shall reap. But you shall sow what is yours to sow, that you may reap what is life's to give, for the seed is in your hand, but the harvest is in life's hand. Sow a

*thought and reap a revelation. Sow a hope
and reap a miracle. Sow a dream and reap a
new life for yourself and perhaps for all the
world. For the world is not a countinghouse,
but a garden, and God is not the keeper of
accounts, but the creative spirit of life bringing forth out of its own infinite will to grow
its ever-renewing, ever-multiplying, ever-pro-
liferating bounty.*

That's the way I feel about sowing and
reaping, karma, predestination, and the law
of cause and effect—the whole deterministic
view of things.

I don't like the notion of a fixed world. I've
been utterly delighted to find in science a
modern theory called Heisenberg's Principle
of Indeterminacy. It's beautiful, like the
speck of yin in the yang, and the speck of
yang in the yin. It states that in the very
nature of the universe there is an element of
uncertainty.

Scientists found, when they got to working
with the basic stuff of things in the subatomic world, they could not accurately
observe what was going on, because their
very act of looking at it disturbed what was
happening. To look they needed light, and the
force of the light waves, striking this sub-

microscopic material, changed its behavior.

I'm happy to accept the belief that the way we look at it affects the behavior of material stuff, though I'm also happy to accept the belief that material stuff affects my thinking.

When we talk about material stuff and thinking, mind-stuff, I think we are talking about the same thing, but we are looking at it from opposite viewpoints. I wonder if we and our world aren't much like a hollow rubber ball. If you push me from the mind-side, from within, my outside world changes, and if you push me from the outside, from the material side, my inner world changes.

So you can't look at anything from too fixed a viewpoint and be sure you see what is really there.

When scientists got to working with subatomic particles, they found these particles did not behave the way they expected them to, the way the law of cause and effect requires. When they looked at one of these particles to find out how fast it was going, when they found out how fast it was going, they couldn't tell where it was; and if they found out where it was, they couldn't tell how fast it was going. They can't say about the smallest particle of the universe, "It's right here," or

"It's moving at such and such a speed." I like this. There is a principle of indeterminacy about the nature of things. So scientists, instead of talking so much about fixed and rigid laws, have turned to talking about probabilities.

This does not mean they've abandoned the notion of scientific law. No, it just means they have a slightly different notion about how the law works. Let's take, for instance, the laws that govern molecular behavior. There are laws, but this does not mean that every molecule reacts according to the laws. No, some molecules don't. Some of them are poets, some are hippies, some are even hippy-poets. But when you're performing an experiment dealing with molecules, you are dealing with multitudes of molecules, and the majority—the vast mass of them—react according to the laws as expected, so that the few who don't obey the laws don't count. Their number is too small to affect the result.

A doctor friend once told me that when he was a young man in college, a great chemist, a Nobel prize winner, lectured his chemistry class. One of the things he remembered the famous scientist saying was that in every experiment there comes a point where there's no way to be sure which way the reaction will go. There's no more reason for it to go one way than the other. But it always goes one way.

This is what Gardner Murphy, for many years with the Menninger Foundation and famous for his work in psychical research, tells us in a paper published in the *Journal of the American Society for Psychical Research*, entitled "Research in Creativeness: What Can It Tell Us about Extrasensory Perception?" He writes:

I once had the good luck to be coming up in the elevator at the Men's Faculty Club at Columbia when Harold Urey, the world-famous Nobel prize winner in chemistry, was explaining to a few of his colleagues an experiment he had just been running. He was asked by one of them about replicating the experiment to see if he got the same results. Well, between the time we left the ground floor and got to the fourth floor, he had given a complete answer. He said, "Yes, you get an interesting result and you take pains to repeat it exactly. You do everything the way you did before and you don't get the same result. And then you say to yourself, 'Ah, I made a little error here and I overlooked something.' And then you change it so that all the little untidy quirks are ironed out and then you do the experiment again. And you get nothing like what you originally got. And then you go back and repeat the entire first experiment again, and you still don't get the same results." And this is the way the Nobel prize winner talks.

But now that I've done my utmost to demolish karma and cause and effect, I hope you'll forgive me if I show a bit of indeterminacy and say I don't want to demolish them. Of course, there is law.

I merely want to enable you to see "it ain't necessarily so." We're not, as so many believe, bound as in a straitjacket, and what will be will be, and we have no power to change what is fated to happen to us. Or as many believe, even more sadly, we've sinned and we must be punished for our sins; we must pay, thought by thought, word by word, act by act, for every evil thought and word and act in this life or any past ones.

I don't believe in such a fixed and fettered world. It makes God into a judgment and an equation instead of the joyous, loving, creative Spirit I feel He has to be. I believe He made us not to be bound by what we have been, but to grow to be what we may be.

Of course, there is law. My reason demands that I accept the fact that there is a law of cause and effect and I am today what I am today because I was what I was yesterday. I have to believe something like this, or abandon reason. But at the same time, my strongest intuitions about myself insist that I am free. I have to believe this, or not only do I lose meaning, but everything there is becomes part of a world that is no more than a blind grinding of atomic gears, where thinking itself is merely the hapless product of this age-long, unthinking process, and meaning is a meaningless word.

But how can I believe that I am free and at the same time believe that I am under law? I have to believe that there are reasons beyond the reach of reason, and there are truths too big and too true to be expressed in one consistent phrase. And I have to believe that I am in the presence of such a truth here, because, however contrary to the rules of logic it may seem, I am ruled by the law of cause and effect, and I am free at the same time. I am dealing with a truth that is a paradox.

I hate to use big words like paradox, but sometimes you have to. A paradox is a statement that seems to say two opposite things, but which may be true.

I have a personal theory. I can't prove it, but it is a strong feeling. Perhaps all the really great truths—the essential universal truths—are paradoxes. They are truths so big we can't grasp them whole, but have to handle them one end at a time.

I even think that, maybe, when you come on a truth completely free of any contradictory elements, you may not have come on much of a truth. You have found only a little truth, or maybe even a half-truth. Emerson said that consistency is the hobgoblin of little minds; perhaps even worse, it is the characteristic of little truths, and a sign you haven't searched long enough and deeply enough.

In the physical world, for instance, does matter consist of particles or of waves? And in the metaphysical world of these lectures, do we have free will or are we governed by the law of cause and effect? Is our self an entity or a process?

There is an ancient law called the Law of the Opposites—I have mentioned it before—that touches on these problems. It holds that if you go far enough in any direction, you will come out in the other direction. Go to one extreme, and you may presently find yourself at the other extreme.

Immanuel Kant in his "Critique of Pure Reason" wrote about four great antinomies. An antinomy is similar to a paradox. It's a proposition that is contradictory, but both its opposing statements can be proved true by our reason.

On the subject of reason, I have always liked Benjamin Franklin's comment that he was glad he was a rational animal, because that enabled him always to find a reason for anything he wanted to believe.

Kant's first antinomy states that the world has a beginning in time and is limited in space, and also the world has no beginning and has no limits. His second says that matter is infinitely divisible and is not infinitely divisible. His third is our familiar one—we have free will and also we are subject to the laws of nature. The fourth states, it is necessary and it is not necessary for there to be a God.

Kant handles his antinomies in a reasonable way by saying that our reason is inadequate to come up with one view about these subjects. Our mind has limits because of the way it is structured. So there are truths beyond our power to grasp entirely and express in words. They are indefinable and ineluctable. In dealing with paradoxes, I seem driven from one big word to yet another.

I've always thought the Buddha handled the ineluctable beautifully. When he was asked about the nature of nirvana—the spiritual state Buddhists hope to attain—he answered, I am sure with a chuckle, "I have not elucidated the *arahat* (one who has attained nirvana) exists after death . . . does not exist after death . . . both exists and does not exist afer death . . . neither exists nor does not exist after death."

So, if you ask me if the self is an entity or a process, if you ask, are we governed by the law of karma, the law of cause and effect, or are we free, I can do as the Buddha and say I haven't said that one or the other is true, that both are true, or that neither is true.

Your answer depends on the direction in which you're looking. There are inside-out and outside-in truths, depending on whether you're looking from center or circumference. If you look from the inside out, from the aspect of eternity, Spinoza's sub specie aeternitatis, where you see what you're looking at in its essential form, I think you'll decide you're an entity. If you look from the outside in, from the standpoint of the passing day, you look more like a process. If you look from the outside in, you see you are governed by the laws of nature. If you look from the inside out, you have no doubt, you are free.

You are a pattern in a pattern. You become what you are because the world is what the world is. And the world becomes what it is because you are what you are. That's the way your self and your life take form.

Maybe the best illustration of what you are like and how you draw your life to you is a magnet. You probably took physics in high school. If you did, one of the first things they gave you was a magnet and some little iron filings and a piece of paper; and then you tapped the paper and held the magnet over it, and the filings and magnet formed a field of force. Likewise, lines of force form between you and the world, and they are always interacting on each other. The magnet in your soul sets up the field of force that is your own, to draw to you the events of your life as if they were iron filings, and shape them into the shape they assume.

What then are we to conclude about the law of sowing and reaping, the law of karma, of cause and effect, and what are we to conclude as to who and what we are?

Imagine a stream. In the stream an eddy forms. Part of the stream, the eddy swirls along, influenced by and influencing the stream, and slowly dissolves into yet another swirling eddy.

Changelessly changing and changingly changeless, we are the stream and we are the eddies that form and dissolve and form again in the stream.

We are what our thoughts and words and acts have made us to be, but we are also what the infinite livingness of life—or God, as I prefer to call it—made us to be—when it made us before time was, or space, before ever the bonds of mind and body were forged. Occasionally, as it struggles to be free, we catch glimpses of this Yet More that is the true ground of our being, changelessly changing and changingly changeless, out of which we form and into which we dissolve to form again and again.

And we see that there is a law of sowing and reaping—call it karma, if you will—but we sow with our own hand and we reap from life's hand, and this is the hand of the Infinite rejoicing in its own creative spontaneity, the

Infinite becoming infinitely more.

The seed we sow may be little more than a handful of dust or a few unlikely-looking pellets, and we may reap barrenness and weeds if we sow in weedy barrenness of soul, but we may also reap a fragrant garden of many-colored flowers, or even of trees that will grow to give shade and fruit and comfort to any who pass by our way.

A Sleep and a Forgetting

Well, that's enough about karma. Let's go
on to other aspects of this subject. A lot of
people say about reincarnation, "We don't
believe in it, because we can't remember our
past lives." That's a very common thought
and it's a sensible one. But the fact is, some,
like General Patton, think they do remember.

My wife, for instance, when she was a little
girl, two or three years old, told her parents,
"My mother and I drowned. We were on a
boat, and the boat sank, and we drowned."
She has told me this was a vivid memory, so
she'd keep repeating it. It irritated her
parents, and they told her to quit saying that,
it wasn't true, she hadn't drowned. But to her
it was a vivid reality. As she grew older the

memory faded, so that now all she can remember is that once she used to say that.

Thousands of persons have had such experiences. They say they remember a former life, and sometimes they describe this life in great detail. Many times we hear reports like that of Shanti Devi, coming from India, and we say, "Well, that's India, and the Hindus believe all this reincarnation stuff." Actually, people in every country have such experiences, and it's not unreasonable that a country like India would be one where many such reports come from. If my wife had been a Hindu and said to her parents what she said, maybe her parents would have paid attention —though Indian parents, when a child starts telling them, "I'm not your child; I'm somebody else's," don't like it any better than my wife's parents did. You can see, that's the sort of thing that would irritate a parent, even if you believe in reincarnation.

There's a well-known scientist at the University of Virginia named Dr. Ian Stevenson. He was head of the department of psychology and neurology there for years, and he's now the professor of psychiatry there. He has made his lifework the scientific investigation of stories of reincarnation. He has studied some 600 cases which have been reported to him, where somebody says, "I remember a former life." He has a staff of scientists, and they go out and investigate any case that's reported to them that they feel worthy of investigation. He has studied cases in many different countries, among them India, Lebanon, Ceylon, Brazil, and Alaska. Interestingly, many Eskimos and American Indians believe they had former lives, which they can remember distinctly.

Stevenson and his staff are scientists. They make every effort to check the testimony of the person who claims to have lived a former life. They check everything in the situation, all the people involved, and the person's statements, to find out if somehow he may be describing a former life because of something he was led to say, or because of something he read, or something he heard, or for any other reason besides really remembering a former life. Stevenson's investigations are thoroughly scientific. Stevenson himself says that he has no conclusive proof of reincarnation, but he's written, among many other papers about it, a book called *Twenty Cases Suggestive of Reincarnation*. (Not available through Unity.) It's quite a book. He took twenty of the cases he thought were most interesting, and he wrote the complete details of his investigation of these cases. All I can say about Stevenson's work is, it's difficult to believe anybody could read his books and articles and not believe there are people who remember former lives.

One interesting thing about his cases, the people who remember a past life—at least the ones he felt were authentic—are usually children. Usually they are very young, and as they grow older, the memory fades, as it did with my wife. In every case, too, the former life was very recent in relation to the present one. Usually only a few years had passed between the end of the life remembered and birth into the present life. Also, usually the person was of the same sex in the former life. That it would be this way makes sense to me. With these conditions, if remembered incidents do well up into the mind, they're more readily related to the present experience. They have a familiarity.

We are all more likely to remember recent events than distant ones, and we're more likely to remember events with which we have some familiarity, events we can associate with something in our present life and world. The principle of association is one memory depends on.

Stevenson says his investigations are not positive proof of reincarnation. Stevenson is a scientist, and he wishes to protect his standing as a research scientist performing a scientific investigation of the facts. But I don't see how you can possibly explain the facts he found out in any other way than by reincarnation.

Some of the most difficult cases to explain by any other means than reincarnation are those involving "xenoglossy." Xenoglossy is the phenomenon where someone speaks or writes in a language foreign to him, which he has never studied, and with which he has no prior acquaintance. There have been many instances of such unaccountable occurrences.

One of the most extraordinary of these involves a girl we know simply as Rosemary. Her story is reported by Dr. Frederick H. Wood, in his book, *After Thirty Centuries,* and a number of other books by him. (Not available from Unity.) Wood reports that he met Rosemary when she had begun to do automatic writing, which disturbed her, and she was referred to him because he knew about such matters. He held many spiritualist sittings with her. In them she claimed to have been an Egyptian named Telika who was a consort of Amenhotep III (1412-1376 B.C.) and she often spoke in Egyptian. Dr. Wood did not know Egyptian, but he wrote down the thousands of words and phrases she uttered as phonetically as he could. These words and phrases have been identified as authentically ancient Egyptian. One has to wonder how a girl who had no way of having any knowledge of ancient Egypt, except at most the popular-magazine knowledge most of us have, could speak ancient Egyptian.

In the last few years, we've had a great deal of hypnotic regression taking place as a means of recalling former existences. Popular interest in it started with the Bridie Murphy case. That really interested a lot of people—they made a best-seller out of it. And a lot of people have tried it since. Stevenson doesn't do hypnotic regression. He simply investigates the facts as he finds the facts. But his facts are very convincing.

Another person who felt he had definite evidence of reincarnation was Edgar Cayce, founder of the Association for Research and Enlightenment. Like Stevenson, Cayce felt people were more likely to remember what had happened to them from one life to another when there was a short time between death and rebirth and when they were of the same sex in both lives.

Wordsworth, the great English poet, in his most famous poem, "Ode On Intimations of Immortality, From Recollections of Early Childhood" intimates much the same thing, in a poetic way.

Our birth is but a sleep and a forgetting:
The Soul that rises with us, our life's
        Star,
    Hath had elsewhere its setting,
    And cometh from afar:
    Not in entire forgetfulness,
    And not in utter nakedness,
But trailing clouds of glory do we come
    From God, who is our home:
Heaven lies about us in our infancy!
Shades of the prison-house begin to close
    Upon the growing Boy,
But he beholds the light, and whence it
        flows,
    He sees it in his joy;
The Youth, who daily farther from the
        east
    Must travel, still is Nature's Priest,
    And by the vision splendid

Is on his way attended;
At length the Man perceives it die away
And fade into the light of common day.

Wordsworth said he didn't just write this poem as a work of his imagination. He wrote it out of his own deep feelings, his own memories, his own experience.

I'm not sure that Wordsworth felt he'd lived before on this earth. But there's no doubt he felt he'd lived before this life. I sense from this poem he felt he'd lived somewhere else, a beautiful place, and he'd brought over a sense of shining, of inspiration. It's interesting, his life carried out the thought he expressed in this beautiful poem. As a young man he wrote some great poetry, but he continued writing till he was eighty—volumes of verse—and he'd have been better off if he'd quit when he was thirty; shades of his prison house had begun to close.

As I said at the beginning of these lectures, in regard to the story of Shanti Devi, I am not going to base the case for reincarnation on stories about people who have been reported to have memories of former lives; too many of us doubt these stories. However, while it may not be reasonable to base the case on them, it is also not reasonable to pay no attention to the reports of scientists like Stevenson and to the hundreds of such cases as have been reported. In almost all these cases there is no reason why the person who tells such a story would tell it except that he really felt he was telling the truth about himself. Perhaps, as Stevenson says, they do not prove reincarnation, but you have to give them serious consideration as evidence suggestive of its occurring. There are too many of them, and they are too hard to explain by other means than reincarnation to disregard.

But to continue on this point of rejecting reincarnation because you can't remember a former life, I say to people, "How much of this life do you remember?"

I wonder, as life recedes into the past, if we remember even one percent of it. That's right. One percent. We have lived twenty-four hours a day for however many years we have lived, and in each of those hours thousands of sensations, feelings, and thoughts have impinged on our consciousness; one percent of them would be a great deal to remember. Most of them passed away immediately. Some stayed with us for a while because they were important at the time. A few may still remain within recall, but precious few!

Most of us retain several thousand words and some of the grammar of our language, and we retain a considerable quantity of facts and skills relating to our special fields. But as to the personal events that happen to us, the thoughts that pass through our minds, the emotions we feel from minute to minute and day to day, most of these we cannot recall. Even the most recent events we are likely to recall only in the vaguest and most general terms. As each year recedes further and further into the past, the events of that year also recede further and further beyond any but vague recall, if even that. In a whole lifetime, years on years, perhaps a few score events stay vivid in memory. No, really to remember —one percent, that's a great deal.

Think about your own life. Can you remember what you were doing ten years ago this date? You may, but it's unlikely. Out of ten thousand persons, maybe one or two can. Can you even remember what you were doing on this date last year? How much do you remember that you were doing last week? Not much. Very, very little. What worries me is, how much are you going to remember of these lectures?

Can you remember anything you were doing on any date ten years ago? How much? You probably can remember some. If you sit down and concentrate, a few things will probably come into your mind that you may be able to place ten years ago. You may be able to. You may not. But, if they do come back, even after only ten years, they come back jumbled together. That's all. You have a heap of memories. It would be very difficult to place them in chronological sequence.

Or when you were five years old, can you remember anything? Usually what we remember from our five-year-old-time is what our parents told us we did. I'm not sure I can remember anything except what my parents loved to tell—stories about my doing this and doing that. Usually something outrageous or ridiculous. When I was five they found something I did amusing and so they told me—and others—about it. That's what Stevenson had to watch with children he investigated, too. Did a parent or relative somehow plant supposed memories in their minds? But with Stevenson's cases the stories are too vivid, too detailed, too different. The subjects he investigated recognized people out of another life; when they were taken to the town in which they said they had lived before, they knew where they had lived. All that sort of thing. Some of the people had marks on them, wounds and the like, that coincided with the story they told about their past life.

But to return to us who have no memory of a former life, how much do we remember of our childhood in this one? At five, four, three, when you were two—I'd say only in extraordinary cases does anyone remember anything he was doing when he was two years old, even though we may say we do. If you do, you're extraordinary. Just as you're extraordinary if you remember anything out of your past life. Obviously, most of us have no such memory. Most of us don't remember any more of our life at two or three than we do about a past one.

My family broke up when I was ten years old, in a very unhappy way. At twenty-two, my father invited me to come back and visit him. He'd like to see his son. I went back, and we passed each other in the street. We didn't know each other. There was no recognition whatever. But then I meet old friends and don't recognize them either. Don't you?

Think about any close friendship that has lasted for more than a few years. How many confidences you have exchanged, how many services you have rendered one another, how many hours of sorrow and joy you have shared, and these bittersweet experiences have left their mark indelibly on your mind and heart. Yes, this I believe—you feel it, don't you? Sometimes the thought of your friend wells up into your consciousness, and you are moved to tears thinking of how much he means to you. Yet how little of the events that passed between you are remembered, except in a misty way.

I have a grandson. He is now twenty years old. When he was three or four years old he was very dear to me. Oh, I don't mean he isn't now. But if you have any teenagers around, you know there is a difference in the way they make you feel. One night, when he was three or four, I was carrying him in my arms. There was a huge full moon in the sky—oh, a glorious round moon—and I pointed it out to him and I kept saying, "Moon, moon," and he'd look up at it and I'd say, "Moon, moon." It was delightful. Then, about two or three weeks later, I was with him walking around in my backyard. It was afternoon, and suddenly he looked up and he pointed and said, "Look, Grandpa, moon!" and I looked, and there was a day moon. Of course, I was delighted that he was smart enough to recognize that pale day moon as the moon I'd pointed out to him. Then he held out his arms and said, "Give it to me, Grandpa." I thought, "I wish I could." That's one of the most vivid memories I have. That moment in that yard, when he was reaching up for the moon. A short time ago we were talking and I told him the story. I said, "Do you remember it, Mike?" He hadn't the slightest memory of it. Not a smidgen. Here's this vivid incident —to me. But not to him. It's gone—though not completely gone, I feel. The mark remains upon our souls, though the memory melts away.

Most of our memories are like that. From my own childhood I remember my grandfather introduced me to Buffalo Bill one time. Buffalo Bill had a circus, and his circus had come to town. My grandfather knew him. He took me up and introduced me to him. You can imagine what a vivid incident that must have been—meeting Buffalo Bill! Now my grandfather and Buffalo Bill are all mixed up in my mind along with King Arthur and Robin Hood and Roland—and Douglas Fairbanks, who probably played all of them. I'm not sure which ones are real and which aren't.

They all swirl about, dissolving into one another like clouds in my memory. That's all.

The past has an unreality about it. A mist falls between us and the past. The mist deepens quickly, so that the figures that move in it through our minds become fantasies, doubtful and indistinct. Which is figure, which is mist becomes harder and harder to make out. And that's not bad. Think about it. What a burden it would be if we remembered all that had happened to us. Frankly, I wish I could forget a few things I can't forget. And I'm fortunate; I let go easily. Some don't. It's like with my own poetry, my own writing. I can't recite any of it from memory. It's hard enough to write it. I sure don't want to go around remembering it. I want you to.

Personally I have never had any memories of some past life. I have never tried to have any as I cannot see how they would contribute to my present unfoldment or happiness. I believe Jesus was right about how we should handle the past. He said: "... *leave the dead to bury their own dead*" (Matt. 8:22).

I am interested in reincarnation not because I want to remember past incarnations —that is the last thing I want. As I have said, I am interested because I want to believe in a meaningful world, and I see no way to explain the events of this life in a just and orderly way except to believe that this life is an episode in an immortal journey.

However, about fifty years ago I had an experience that has ever since made me wonder if possibly it was connected with a former existence.

Some friends and I had joined the YMCA. While we were there, a fencing class began and we joined it. The class did not last long, as most of its members quickly lost interest; fencing is an arduous, demanding sport.

I quickly found I had some ability at it, but that is not the point of this story. As I dueled with various opponents, I found that I had an amazing and unexpected skill. As we thrust and parried, suddenly I would find that my sword, as I drew it back, was bringing with it the sword of my opponent, and he stood before me disarmed. Now I did not have the slightest idea how I did this. But to my delight and my opponent's chagrin, I would find it happening. Our teacher was interested, but I could not show him how I did it as I did not know how I did it, and I could not do it at will. It would happen, that is all.

In modern fencing, there is no advantage in

disarming your opponent. It does not score a point for you. The judges merely stop the contest until your opponent has regained his sword.

But think what it once would have meant, when you were fighting for your life. I can think of no skill that would be more precious. I must admit, this made me wonder—did I once, in some forgotten life, know how to do this? For various reasons, as you may imagine, I am just as glad I cannot remember.

What Do We Remember?

Most people who believe in reincarnation believe we wipe out the memory of our former life somewhere during the interval between death and rebirth. Among the ancients, Plato and Virgil wrote descriptions of the afterworld. Both of them believed in reincarnation, and both of them described the soul as retaining the memory of this life until the time comes for its reentry into our world. Then the soul drinks from the waters of the river called Lethe or Forgetfulness, all memory disappears, and the soul is ready to be incorporated in another body.

If you believe the stories of those who say they've communicated with their dead, you have to assume that the dead remember their life here on earth—they return to people who were dear to them; obviously, they remember them. And they speak of incidents that occurred when they were here.

But if this is so, and reincarnation is a fact, why don't we remember our former life after we're reborn?

This question of memory—or rather, the lack of it—is the principal reason why those who don't believe in reincarnation don't believe in it—except for those who don't believe in it simply because it wasn't one of the beliefs they were brought up in.

If we believe in reincarnation, we have to believe, somewhere between death and rebirth, the memories are wiped out.

To me, it would seem most reasonable to assume that after death the memories of this life recede gradually, just as they do here. It would be natural for this to occur. It would occur much more swiftly than here, because there would be little or nothing occurring in another life that would require us to recall events in this one.

How does memory work? What does it consist of? Words or pictures, doesn't it? We think in words and pictures—or, oops! I forgot—mathematical symbols. So a memory may be a name, or a series of words or symbols that embody an idea or a bit of information, or it may be a still or moving picture. Or it may be mathematical symbols.

We call these words or pictures that represent past knowledge, events, or people into our minds mainly because we need them to help us to handle something we're presently working on, or some event occurs that conjures them back into our minds through the process of association.

Association is probably the principal way the mind works. Like produces like. Not only birds, but thoughts of a feather flock together. It's through systematically developing methods of association that memory experts produce their marvelous feats of memory.

Thousands of stimuli register on our minds continually; hundreds of events happen to us in a day. Most of these pass almost immediately from memory. Only those incidents and bits of knowledge that are of great importance or are deeply impressed on our minds by their emotional vividness stay with us even for a brief time. Interestingly—and paradoxically—as psychoanalysts have proved, when an event is accompanied by too vivid an emotion, it may be instantly wiped out of mind.

This may be a point to bear in mind in thinking about why we may not remember our former life. We don't know what powerful emotional experiences may occur with dying, with life after death, and with rebirth. Could there be experiences in this in-between world that literally shock our past life out of our minds? It's a thought!

To me, however, as I've said, the most reasonable explanation is that our memories vanish between lives just as they do during this one, only quicker, because there would be little or nothing in the afterlife to be associated with this one. Whatever events may occur in a spirit world to bodiless beings are bound to be different than events in this material space-time world where we think of ourselves mainly as physical bodies, and most of our experiences come to us through our body's physical, sensory apparatus.

Also, just as it does here, the loss of memory would occur in different individuals at different rates and in different degrees. Some would quickly let go all memory of this life; others might retain many memories for a long while—perhaps, as is apparently the case with those who recall incidents of a former life, even into the next life.

To show how elusive memory is about things in this world, let me use myself as an example, though you may be fully aware of this from the difficulty you have remembering things you wish you could remember. But let's consider me in relation to my poetry, a very important part of my life.

I write a poem. It comes to me line by line, sometimes a couple of lines, sometimes a few lines more. If I don't write them down immediately—and I mean immediately!—I may lose them. Yes, lose them. I can't recall them. I've had it happen—much to my regret, because nothing is more important to me. Two minutes may be too long; my mind goes leaping creatively from new phrase to new phrase, and if I don't put it down as it comes, my mind rushes on and won't come back.

This is a thought, too. If after I've died I'm going to live again, my mind must be in a very creative mood, busy creating the new me. It's not going to turn back from this intense activity—if you've done creative work, you know how intense it is—to recall its past. If it didn't get written down, it's gone. Why would sensory details that are never going to be repeated get written down?

But this again is just passing conjecture about the next life. Let's return to my poems and my remembering them in this life. When I've finally finished a poem, it makes a deep impression on me. I read it over and over, hoping to make it better. I repeat the lines to myself, I type it out, maybe several times. It may even appear in print. I may recite it to many audiences. So it would appear to be sharply etched in my memory. Yet I don't keep my poems in memory, or even within easy recall, sometimes not even after I've repeated them hundreds of times. Sometimes I not only have difficulty remembering them, but remembering I wrote them. As for other people's poetry—as you might know would be true of a poet—I remember it even more poorly.

Because I write and speak, I often have a need to quote or at least to remember the substance of some piece of writing, so I have a special incentive to remember. I have unusual powers of recall. On occasion I've memorized great masses of writing, and it isn't too hard for me to do this. I've even memorized hour-long speeches in foreign languages in which I have almost no fluency.

But almost instantly, when the need for any of this material passes, the lines I've so laboriously fixed in my mind pass with the need.

My friends think I have unusual powers of recall because so many facts in so many different fields, often trivial, hang loosely in my mind and sometimes bob to the surface. But the truth is I have the usual trouble remembering names and faces. I've observed, even in fields I've researched deeply and taught for years, once I no longer teach them, the details fade, and the only way I can recall them is to reread my notes or, where my notes aren't complete enough, I have to reread the books from which I originally garnered the material.

I believe the main cause of memory is incentive; we have to have a reason for remembering. The main factor in memory is repetition; we bring it to mind over and over. Usually we do this because we have a need to do this, or through association.

Once we pass out of this life and it becomes apparent we won't be able to renew the associations we've had or to use the knowledge we've acquired, at least for a long time, there's every reason to believe that the memories connected with people, knowledge, and events we have no further use for would quickly fade.

Some psychologists believe that every incident, no matter how trivial, every sensation, no matter how lightly received, is recorded by the brain as we experience it, although it immediately passes from conscious memory. This belief has been heightened by the ability of hypnotists to bring back events a person has no conscious recollection of. If this is true, even partly true, then everything we've ever done or have ever been is recorded on our soul, not to be drawn into conscious memory, but to influence and direct and assist us to be and do what we find ourselves having to be and do now. This could explain much that's hard to explain in terms of this life only.

I have observed that though details fade rapidly from my memory once they are no longer used, let the need for them arise again—as when I need to relearn a forgotten language because I have to speak it again, or I need to relearn names, dates, and details of a subject because I have to make new lectures on it, or I need to play a game I quit playing years ago—even after a lapse of many years, it is amazing how quickly the forgotten skills and materials reemerge in the mind. Sometimes it is as if they suddenly appear—there they are as I call upon them.

Relearning is not at all like learning the first time. It is almost like a fan unfolding. You reach into the drawer of your mind where you stored it and draw it forth, and how speedily how much you thought forgotten unrolls before you. Could this not explain why all of us have certain fields of knowledge that are easier for us to learn than others? Once, we knew them.

We're born with unequal talents and abilities. This has seemed especially to be true in fields like music. I think it would logically follow that this might be the case. Creative talent as a musician or a composer wouldn't depend on the prior accumulation and retention of great stores of detailed information, such as might be needed, say, by a historian or an engineer. As a performer, a musician may need the ability to hold whole pieces of music note by note in his mind, but his creative powers depend more on a sense of rhythm and a feeling for melody and harmony.

These don't depend on memory, but are clearly imbedded in the unconscious layers of our being. We just say of someone, "He was born with them," which is true. Training may sharpen them. That's all. They're gifts we brought with us at birth.

I suppose you can explain such gifts in terms of heredity and genetics, but then you have to explain heredity and genetics. What shapes our genetic inheritance? It seems to me, a past life is a very reasonable explanation for the different talents and abilities we may be born with.

If our whole past is recorded on our soul, though beyond the reach of conscious memory, how likely it would be that it would be the most powerful influence on us imaginable, and would drive us to do the things we do and become the person we become.

Let me make clear, I am not saying that our being a musician or an engineer in this life means that we will be a musician or engineer in the next one. It may even mean that we will want to be anything but a musician or engineer.

We may be working to develop elements in ourselves and our lives that will press us to continue unfolding in the same direction we have taken this time, or we may want and need an entirely different kind of experience.

The law of life is the law of growth. What

do we need to meet the challenges and make the growth that is ours to make? What have we come up to?

I would assume that the same factors at work in this life will be at work in any other life. What motivates us, whether consciously or unconsciously, to become what we have become now? Is it not the needs of our soul and the longings of our hearts?

There is one other extremely important factor—the world we are born into, the physical and cultural environment we find ourselves in. This obviously limits our choices and may dictate the direction in which we have to grow, whether we will or not.

The fact that most of us don't remember the details of our former lives isn't sufficient reason for not believing in reincarnation. As I've said, we don't remember much of this one, yet that doesn't interfere with our living it meaningfully and enjoyably. In fact, if our minds were cluttered by constant awareness of the thousands on thousands of events we've experienced in this life, we probably couldn't bear to live, let alone have a meaningful life. Our mind would be pandemonium and chaos.

No, our ability to obliterate most of our

past—all we don't need—is a fortunate gift. It enables us to live an orderly and progressive existence.

When you really think about it, our inability to remember a past life is a merciful provision.

Of what value would such a memory be? It would merely clutter our thought with worthless and unrelated material that would keep us from concentrating on what we have to do now, which is, live day by day in a progressive way.

Everything about the way mind works is designed to enable us to do this—to concentrate on the task at hand. Mind is designed so that we can pay attention to only one thing at a time.

So let's give thanks that memory is elusive and at best provides us only with the recollection we need to live the life we have to live now.

Personality, Individuality

Memory is not the all-important all, the without-which-we're-not, that we sometimes get to thinking it is. It's easy to get to thinking we're a bundle of memories, but that's only part of us.

Occasionally someone suffers amnesia and forgets everything about his prior personal life. But that doesn't make him not be. He—what he really is—goes right on, just as much a living being as he was before, and he builds a new existence. He may not remember the life he lived or who he was before, but that doesn't mean he has ceased to be, nor does it mean that he is not the same individual he was before he forgot who he was. If you are close to someone like this, you may feel how changed his actions and reactions are, and how many parts of his previous nature have passed away with the passing of his memories. But you do not feel that he is not the same individual; he has just changed his nature, that is all.

You can see even more clearly in the case of multiple personalities how much more than memories we are. Psychologists have reported a number of these interesting cases, sometimes where the individual is two persons, sometimes where he is many, all with very different reactions and different relations to the other personalities, and to other individuals. In these cases sometimes one personality remembers what the other has done; sometimes it does not remember. But the individual is the individual, whether or not one of his personalities remembers what it has done or what the other has done. Memories, important as they are, are not what makes us what we are. There is that which is what we are, whether it remembers its past life or not.

You may say, "Ah, but we consider it to be one person because, whatever the varying personalities are doing, they are all manifesting in one physical body and using the same set of physical faculties." This may be true, but how true is it? Like Dr. Jekyll and Mr. Hyde, the different personalities may use different voices; they may have very different appearances, comb their hair differently, have different expressions on their face, wear different clothes; they may be of different ages; they may even be of different sexes; and, as I say, the one may not even know of the other's existence.

But they are one individual.

When we see individuals with multiple personalities, and when we see one personality not remember any of his experiences when he is another, we have to ask how important memory is. Also we have come again to the question: What are we? When we refer to ourselves, what do we mean by self? When we say someone is a person, what is a person?

Sometimes we use words like *self* and *person* in a limited sense to mean the particular body and personality we appear to be to ourselves, our friends, and acquaintances now. But sometimes when we use them, we have a strong sense of something more, of something very hard to place limits on and define.

At any rate, in such cases, we clearly see that we are more than a bundle of memories;

our memories are just a part of what we are.

Stop and think about yourself. The greatest part of you, of what you are, is the unconscious area of your being. You're a house of many rooms, and you don't even know what's going on in most of them.

All kinds of things are going on in you all the time. Once in a great while they pop up into consciousness as thoughts and feelings, impulses and desires, but you're not just the you you're conscious of. You are much more than that. Much more! Sigmund Freud pointed this out to us very clearly—there's more to our unconscious than our conscious nature—we're all kinds of things that we don't know we are. Ever since Sigmund Freud, a veritable mob, not only of psychologists, but also playwrights, novelists, poets, priests, preachers—and friends and neighbors, if we let them—have been endlessly telling us how important our unconscious nature is, and gladly helping us to probe it.

However, we don't need psychologists to tell us. I don't believe there's ever been a human being who hasn't felt it in himself. You feel it. There's more to you than anything you've ever been, more than everything on the surface you seem to be. Much more!

We all have a secret soul. Occasionally we commune with it. We are driven by needs and impulses, reluctances and yearnings, fears and animosities, and passions and attachments that rarely find expression in terms of conscious thinking, but they are there—sometimes painfully, sometimes gloriously, there! They are the true shapers and molders of our lives. Sometimes they make one of us into a saint, sometimes into a monster. But all the time they are driving all of us to be what we come to be. *For as he thinketh in his heart, so is he* (Prov. 23:7, A.V.). The key words here are *in his heart,* that is, in the core of his being, not on the conscious surface, but in his largely unconscious deeps.

Here, in these deeps of us, are the real springs of our present life and actions. Here is our true nature; this is where we operate from—from the self we're hardly conscious of.

Some people go through life with little understanding that they are more than what they seem to be on the surface. They don't know what makes them do what they're doing.

Maybe you like apple pie; maybe you don't. But you don't know why, probably. Maybe you like blondes and maybe you don't. Maybe you like elm trees, maybe you like oaks; maybe you don't like trees. But if somebody asked you why, you'd have a hard time telling them. No, most of you lies in unconscious areas of your nature. What we are conscious of, what we hold in memory, these are a relatively small part of what we are.

For instance, we can't remember our dreams, or if we can, how many of them do we remember? At best a handful. But dreams— our life of dreams—that's a very important part of our life. A very important part. Stop and think how much you dream. We sleep, let's say, eight hours a night. But nobody is conscious of eight hours of dreams when he wakes in the morning. Most of the time I can't recall eight minutes of dreams or even eight seconds.

Experts say you don't dream eight hours. You only dream about four hours. They think they can tell by measuring whether your eyelids are flicking or not; they call this REM, rapid eye movement sleep. They think you are dreaming only during REM sleep, when your eyelids are flicking. Let's admit they're right. The ancients taught there is both dreaming and dreamless slumber.

So, all you had last night were four hours of dream life. But who can recall four hours of dreams? Yet you've had—how old are you?—all these years of dream life—and how many minutes of it can you remember? Any? And no one knows, maybe in dreamless slumber your dreams just run deeper, that's all, more buried and perhaps more important to you than the ones you occasionally remember. I know I dream—all of us do, don't we? We awake and we know we dreamed, but for the life of us we often can't remember what we dreamed. Even if we try, we can't pull it up into consciousness. Can we be sure that all of our life is not a dream?

I've always liked the piece by a great Chinese writer—maybe he was the best of all Chinese writers—Chuang tze, and he lived, I think, about 300 years after Lao-tzu who founded Taoism. He wrote beautiful essays, and in one of them he says: *Once upon a time I, Chuang tze, dreamt I was a butterfly, fluttering hither and thither, to all intents and purposes a butterfly. Suddenly, I awaked. Now I do not know whether I was then a man dreaming I was a butterfly, or whether I am now a butterfly dreaming I am a man.*

It's a pretty good question. I've always felt

227

that if we did remember another life we've had, it would seem like a dream, a fantasy. That would be the only way it could be. As it ran through our minds, we'd think, "It's something I dreamed." That's the way all our past is.

People have a vivid experience; it may be happy, it may be unhappy, and a short time afterward you hear them say, "That's all like a dream now. Just a dream." And so it is. All the past is like a dream. Once past, it exists only in mind.

My grandfather was probably the dearest memory of my childhood. But I never saw him after I was ten, and if you asked me what he looked like, all I can recall is, he had a big white mustache, and I'm not sure of its shape. To me he was a giant of a man. But my mother told me he was only five feet two inches tall.

What is the past except something we hold in mind? Our minds tell us of this or that event, "This really happened." That's all we have—testimony of our minds. But that's all we had when it was happening—the testimony of our minds. That's all we ever have.

People ask, "What happens when we die? What is the nature of life after death?" As

I've said before, many people have described the next life and they have given us different descriptions. One reassuring point, if the descriptions reported by those who've died and returned to life—those who've had near-death experiences—have validity, there's nothing to be afraid of. Their experiences have all been reassuring. I believe that; there's nothing to be afraid of.

Most modern writers about the next life leave us, for the most part, with a notion of an insubstantial, vaporous existence in an insubstantial, vaporous world. We are spirits, that's all, waiting to live fully again. Somehow the thought of being spirits has never had much reality for most of us. We are a bunch of unshriven materialists, or perhaps, I might better say, realists.

Our language shows how true this is. Our word *real* comes from the Latin word, *res*, which means "thing." When we say of something, "It's real," we mean it has material substance, it's flesh and blood, it's sticks and stones. When we say that someone just thought it, or when we say of something, "It's just a thought," we are almost saying it is not real. The same goes for ideas like spirit and soul. We say you can see right through spirits and ghosts, and we probably don't mean just with our eyes.

So when people describe the next world and tell us we are going to be spirits, we and the next world take on an intangible, nebulous quality—at least, to most of us.

The Hindus make a tremendous effort to deny the reality of the material world, but their attempt to describe spiritual worlds shows how bound to material notions even the most unworldly of us are likely to be. To picture the difference between this world and the next, they tell this story. Imagine the happiest prince in the world. He's just won the world's richest kingdom. He's conquered his deadliest foes in personal combat and put all their armies to flight. He's just wed the world's most beautiful princess. Now he mounts his throne, surrounded by his loyal subjects, loading him with gifts and shouting his praises. The happiness of the meanest inhabitant of the next higher level of consciousness is ten thousand times greater than that of this prince. Can you imagine a more materialistic spirituality?

Most ancient people describe the next world in quasi-physical terms. Thus, the Greeks depicted Hades as having various levels, from Tartarus, where bad shades were subjected to very physical tortures, to Elysium, where the good were close to the gods and wandered in much less vividly detailed ways. Interestingly, as I've said, the Greek afterworld had its plain of forgetfulness through which runs the river Lethe, whose water we must drink before we're reborn upon the earth.

Different Christian churches have different teachings about the next life. The basic Catholic doctrine, I believe, is based on Aristotle's teaching that the soul cannot have an independent existence from the body. Soul and body are linked. Therefore, when you die, you go into a state of complete oblivion. You experience nothing until the Day of Judgment, and at that time soul and body are joined together and are resurrected. I believe that's the doctrine of a number of Christian churches.

But in the popular belief, when you die you're going to be judged right then and dragged off to hell or lifted up to heaven.

But whether we have bodies or are only spirits, our bliss and torment are pictured in physical terms. In most of the great classic descriptions of the world, heaven and hell are very earthy places. Thus the heaven of the early church fathers was a cozy, comfortable place of pearly gates and golden streets, where the saints could sit on the wall and gleefully look down at those who had tormented them on earth, being tormented now in their turn. Dante in "The Divine Comedy" described a world of rewards and punishments that seemed just and desirable to his time and culture—and most of all, to him. Mohammed, weary of the desert, described paradise as a place of springs and fountains, a place for feasting and wine—forbidden on earth—a place for consorting with the houris. The houris are beautiful maidens, "with large dark eyes, like pearls hidden in their shells," and they are ever virgin.

Most of the people who believe in reincarnation have also believed in heavens and hells. They don't make them permanent, that's all. You're not going someplace and be there forever. The most popular Buddhist sects, for instance, Shin and Jodo, believe there's a lovely heaven and there's a Buddha who made it, and all you have to do is believe in that Buddha and repeat his name, *Namu Omito Fo,* Hail, Amitabha Buddha, and he'll see that you get in. You can't stay there forever, however; you have to come back and try again here on earth.

It's only Christians and Moslems who make heaven and hell last forever. This is interesting, too. Most of the East believes that, in order to gain the state of spiritual perfection that is the end and goal of existence—they have many names for it—call it what you want—*moksha,* nirvana, *samadhi, turiya*—you've got to come back here on earth and make your overcoming here. Almost all of them believe this. Take the Buddha, for instance, Gautama Siddhartha. There are many Buddhas, but Gautama Siddartha is the man who founded the religion. After many incarnations, he had become a divine being in one of the Buddhist heavens. But in order for him to gain perfect enlightenment and become the savior—the Buddha— he had to come back here on earth and be born as Gautama Siddhartha. So he came back.

The East believes even the gods—they have many gods—but even the gods are also under the law of karma and they have to reincarnate sooner or later and work out the karma which made them gods.

As for myself, the exact nature of the next

world has never concerned me. I'm willing to let the details unfold as I reach them, just as I have in this one. I can understand how Thoreau felt when he lay dying and a friend, leaning over him, asked him: *"Henry, you are so near the border now, can you see anything on the other side?"* and Thoreau whispered, *"One world at a time, Parker, one world at a time."*

I believe I have lived before; I believe I will live again. But who I was and who I will be have never concerned me. Somehow I think it will take care of itself as this life has. The next world will be my world, a world where I can be me, just as this world has been. As I've said, like Emerson, what I have seen teaches me to trust my Creator in what I have not seen.

I think part of me knows, but it's that part of me that's deeper than my daily self, and I cannot draw it forth in words. I have no description, but here is what I have written about it:

Seafarers all, we came hither in a ship no man remembers, by a course no man can chart on any map. Not by sails our ship was driven over this sea, nor with oars, nor on wings like a ship of the air. For this deep, from which we drew, is deeper than space. All the worlds of space are but an island in this ocean. Yet it is no unfamiliar deep; nor are its courses unknown, though they are uncharted. Its mysteries are graven in our inmost self. Without remembering, we know its ways as the migratory plover knows its way through the trackless air. No one has to tell us how to go, as no one has to tell the salmon or the eel. No star need shine in the sky for us to reckon our course by. Our light is in ourself. There will be tempests, but we are stronger than tempest—and the calm is in our soul, not in the sea. There will be night, but we are children of the light. We were meant for the deep, not for the shallows. We came out of it. We return into it. It is our native element, a spiritual dimension. We are spiritual beings and were made for soul-faring.

Many people who think about reincarnation are concerned as to where and how it may take place. They ask, "Do we have to reincarnate back here on earth?" Charles Fillmore, who cofounded Unity, felt we did. He had strong feelings about this. He was certain we reincarnated and certain we were re-embodied here. He used to tell us in Unity, "All of us have been together many times.

We've reached a similar level of consciousness, and are working out the same things." He felt that people of like mind were drawn together and would be drawn together again. He had strong feelings about this. We reincarnate here.

Also Edgar Cayce of A.R.E. thought we have to reincarnate here. He felt we had reached the plane of consciousness represented by the earth, and we would remain here until we had risen to a higher level of spiritual development.

I can see the reasonableness of this idea that we will reincarnate here as long as we are of the earth earthy. The level of consciousness that drew me here this time will draw me here again—unless I've moved to some other level of consciousness. And it will draw me again to the people on my level, the people I am linked to, mentally and emotionally and spiritually. As long as we're working out problems with one another, and maybe between one another, that seems a reasonable notion.

But I don't know. It's a big world, with galaxy on galaxy and star on star and sun on sun and planet on planet. Scientists have found billions of stars just in the galaxy in which we live, the Milky Way; and they have found billions of galaxies beyond our own; and they believe that many of these billions on billions of stars that revolve in the billions on billions of galaxies have planetary systems like our own star's, the sun. So I don't know. It's reasonable to believe I may be drawn back here, but it's also reasonable to believe that there are many worlds on which I might be born. Who can say that this space-time mode of manifestation is the only one in which I may find expression?

I think many people have a sense that somehow this is not their only world, not even their native world. This is not often more than a vague feeling, but if you think about it, you may find that you sometimes have such a sense. I love this world. You can't write poetry the way I have and not love the world. I'm so aware of its beauty— this windy, watery, blue-green globe I live on! It's a beautiful place and I love it deeply. But I feel that, dear as it is, it's only an inn, only my present place of sojourning. I came here, and at last I'll travel on.

I wrote a piece about this. I'll read it to you. I hope you don't mind my reading these things. I enjoy reading them and I think I say it better when I write than when I'm talking.

Is there anyone who's never driven down a road and suddenly the country he was driving through was not the country lying round about him but a strange and different country? Yet for all its suddenness and unexpectedness, not an unexpected country. It's almost as if you somehow came up over the hills that hem round the mind and there, spreading out before you, was the native valley of the soul—warm, dear, shining, bringing always a sense of homecoming, always an intimation of perfection, always a feeling that you are about to go back where you belong, a sense of being for a moment in a world far more real and more familiar than the world of every day. It's always only for a moment— and in a moment you're driving back in the world of every day. A trick of the mind, you say, and dismiss it. But is every day less a trick of the mind, less a state of awareness? Or are there doors and windows in the mind that once in a while—who knows how or why —we open and find ourselves staring into worlds we knew were there but had for a time forgotten? I know past any doubting that this world where now I find myself is not the country of my origin. Dearly as I love it, I am but an immigrant.

Perhaps that's why I love it so much. All I know is this: I've lived before and I will again. That's all that's important. This is the world I've come up to. And the next world will be the world I've come up to, the world I can exist in and can grasp at my level of awareness.

Now I'll read you another piece about that:

Life did not begin with birth; we have come through aeons of experience beyond imagining. And here we are. In this! In this delightful, sometimes frightful, aching, delicious world!

You are on your way. Your way may carry you to strange and curious scenes, perhaps. Sooner or later, no doubt it will.

But whether it be a world of green skies and purple seas, of fields that lie on edge and hollow hills, or have no skies or seas or fields or hills at all, if thoughts find form and form becomes like thoughts there—still it will be a world where you will be at home.

It will be your world, a world where you can exist, a world that you can grasp and lay hold of in your mind, and with your heart; a world —I have faith—where you can, as you have here, grow to be more than you have been.

What then do I believe survives? Since it's obvious that conscious memory doesn't survive—except in rare cases—the part of us that does survive must be a part that lies beyond our conscious self.

Most Christian religions speak of that which survives as Spirit or soul. The two words are usually used interchangeably. However, as I pointed out, the new metaphysical religions make a distinction between the two.

Many people who believe in reincarnation argue that only Spirit, the perfect God-image, the one, true, changeless, and eternal Self, survives. Others hold that the soul also survives and is reincarnated. Then there is the Buddha who does not teach that you are Spirit, soul, or self, but believes that the eddy in the world-sea of being out of which you arose this time, though it dissolves, is setting into movement the sea currents that will once again whirl the separate components of your being, the *skandhas,* into existence as you.

Spirit and soul are good words, but they have been used in ways that give them ghost-like qualities, which reincarnation does not need. Though I like the Buddha's notion that we're more process than entity, I do believe we have a real self.

Perhaps the best word is individuality. It is a word used by many persons who discuss reincarnation. It is not connected with any particular theology. It enables the user to indicate that he is speaking of an aspect of being that is more than personality.

Personality is that which we seem to be—to ourselves and to others. We may be introverted or extroverted, agressive or shy, proud or humble, brave or fearful, quiet or talkative, miserly or generous, and so on; we may demonstrate certain special skills and abilities. Individuality includes not only qualities we are conscious of, but the basic traits, attitudes, and tendencies that lie at the root of our conscious thoughts, words, and actions. In other words, that which makes us what we are and determines how we act.

I don't like to use this analogy, because if there's anything we all too human creatures are not like, it's an iceberg. But we are like it in that only the merest tip of our being appears above the surface. Our conscious personality, important as it is, and revealing as it is—sometimes especially revealing because of what it contrives to conceal, not only from others but from ourselves—is the mere tip of the iceberg of self. Perhaps a better simile would be to liken us to a volcano. We're the smoking cinder cone we see from the surface, but we're also the fiery rivers of lava that bubble up from molten seas of magma in the deeps.

But we're not volcanoes or icebergs. We're the living creative children of the Creative Principle of Life.

What are you in your heart? It is this that will give you the form you will have beyond death. Call it spirit, mind, *atman, purusa,* individuality, let it be by way of process or as an entity, what survives, if it is meaningful to me, must be me.

I don't believe the conscious personality called Jim Freeman survives. But the real self of me that in this time and place is putting forth the pattern of thoughts and words and deeds that this time around answers to the name Jim—this survives, and will put forth yet other patterns of thoughts and words and deeds, as much me as I am now. At the root of my life are the basic elements of my being, and these abide and grow. Ah, there's a thought more to my liking than volcanoes and icebergs—my root being!

For am I not much like a perennial plant? With spring, my root being, which lay mostly dormant through the winter, quickens with life and puts forth stem and branch and leaf and flower. Then, with the return of winter, my root being draws into itself whatever was of more than seasonal value, and waits once more for spring. The flowering plant we see withers and becomes but dust, but am I not even more the immortal root? This lives on and on, and contains within itself the essence of what I am and what I may become. Nothing true of me is lost. All that I am capable of being is there, contained in my root being hidden in the underground of my nature. From this root of my being, I come forth again and again, always the same, yet never the same, the same perennial plant, but always flowering anew.

Transmigration

Before we go any further, let me take up a subject that bothers many people when they hear someone talk about reincarnation. They don't like the idea because they think it means they may have to come back as animals. Usually when we refer to the belief that human beings may come back as animals, we use the word *transmigration*. Reincarnation usually refers to the belief that we return in human form.

Unity teaches that we are human beings and will always be human beings, never animals. As far as I know, all the schools in the Western world that teach reincarnation believe you come back in human form. As far as I know, all the Eastern religions teach that you may return as an animal, as a plant—or even as a god, if you're lucky enough and good enough; that is, if your karma has brought you to godhood.

I don't know how seriously a Buddhist or Hindu takes the possibility that he might actually return as an animal. Perhaps the belief is like many musty items in the theological cupboard of every religion; the followers of the religion know it is there, but don't consider it as relating to them. I believe a Hindu would think he could only return as an animal if he had lived a life so animalistic that it justified his returning as an inferior creature. However, in the Jataka tales, a collection of stories that relate the former lives of the Buddha as he grew toward sainthood, it is often as an animal that he works out his destiny. The doctrine of ahimsa—reverence for life, noninjury to all living forms—lies deeply rooted in the heart of all the great Eastern religions, and it is an adornment, not a blemish. Christianity has made it an endearing quality of some of our best-loved saints, like Francis of Assisi.

All ancient people accepted the fact that they might be re-embodied in animal, or even in plant form. Our ancestors lived close to nature and didn't have the great feeling of superiority and even disdain for animals that we have. We're pretty much separated from nature except when it flies in through the window or crawls across our floor. Our ancestors weren't so sealed off from other forms of life. Animals of all kinds were all around them, and our ancestors could see how much like themselves animals were. They felt akin, they had no trouble feeling they and animals had family ties with one another, and they expressed these in totemic symbols. It wasn't hard for a clan or tribe to think of some special animal as the tribe's ancestor. It wasn't hard to think of the soul as passing at death into the body of an animal, and vice versa. Some felt the soul chose alternate forms, one time as a human being, a member of the tribe, and the next time as the tribal animal.

This close relationship is shown in many fairy tales where a prince or princess is changed into animal form and has to be changed back. All of us know the story of Beauty and the Beast and of the frog prince who has to be kissed by the beautiful princess, but there are hundreds of such stories. And more grisly forms of the belief exist, in which human beings are vampire bats and werewolves and the like.

As I say, our ancestors didn't feel so different or so superior to other forms of life. They knew how superior animals were to them in so many ways.

We moderns are prone to forget we are animals. But whatever else we may believe we are and however superior we may think we are, we are also animals. Biologists, even if they're Catholic priests or Protestant fundamentalists, classify us as belonging to the kingdom of Animalia, of the phylum Chordata, the subphylum Vertebrata, the class Mammalia, the order Primates, the suborder Anthropoidea, the family Hominidae, the genus Homo, the species Homo sapiens. I don't believe there is any biologist, no matter how religious he might be, who wouldn't say this is a scientific description of man—yes, and of woman, too.

This doesn't mean we're not also spiritual beings. I believe we are spiritual beings living in a spiritual world, but also I can't doubt that we're physical beings living in a physical world. As I've said, all great truths are paradoxes and I don't find these two conditions mutually exclusive.

I suppose I don't have difficulty thinking of myself as an animal, not only because I'm a child of the scientific age and so was taught this in my high school biology class, but also perhaps I'm more a child of nature than many of my fellow Homo sapiens, and don't feel very superior to other animals or even to plants.

I have asked myself, how are we human beings superior to other species? For one thing, we have a power of abstract reasoning they don't seem to have. Also, though animals can be very loving and can selflessly sacrifice themselves for one another—or for us when we are dear to them—we human beings have a wonderful quality I don't think I've ever seen in an animal. We are capable of mercy.

I have never seen an animal stop from pursuing its prey or attacking its enemy just because it was suddenly moved with pity. We human beings are capable of this. We can spare those we don't like and forgive our enemies, even those who would destroy us, had they the power.

Let me tell you a silly story about mercy.

I don't like starlings. I don't like them at all. They strut in gangs across the lawn, crowd one another from the feeders, and drive away birds I like. There are two large maple trees in front of my house that are starling hotels. In the winter when it gets cold and snowy, the starlings gather in a circle around the top of my fireplace chimney whenever I have a fire going. I can accept this, except that once in a while one of them has fallen down the chimney into the fire.

I still remember the first time I became aware that one of them had committed this zany awkwardness. When I saw the bird frantically flitting about amid the flames, though I may have secretly thought, "Good, one less starling," I opened the firescreen and tried to rescue it. Naturally, the bird tried to avoid my clutch, and the two of us flailed about in the flames. I realized it was a foolish act. I could catch fire, the two of us could knock hot coals into the room, or the bird could catch fire, dart past me into the room, and set the house afire. But I wildly persevered until I had the bird safely in hand. There it lay utterly still. I decided the shock had been too great. I carried it out and laid it down in the snow. Instantly with a whoosh it was up in the air. I watched it rise, fly about, then take its place in the circle at the top of the chimney. I could hear it squawkingly describing its adventure to the rest of the flock. There was no question as to what I heard it saying: "I was in hell. The devil had me in his hand, but I got away."

The quality of mercy! We are capable of mercy—even toward those we don't like, even toward our enemies. I don't think any other species except our human one has this beautiful trait. It is one we can take pride in. We are capable of mercy!

Mercy, however, is not a quality we display too much of the time. Mainly we have demonstrated our superiority to animals as killers. We've been able to kill them more effectively than they've been able to kill us. And sad to say, we've done it.

In my book, *Love, Loved, Loving* (out of print), I have a piece entitled "Who Is King of the World?" about an animal and a plant who find themselves living together in a small place that is theirs alone. The animal eats the fruit of the plant, but the plant doesn't mind; it produces its fruit to be eaten. But the animal gets to thinking how superior it is to the plant, and demands that when it approaches, the plant must bow down and prostrate its branches to the ground. The plant is a gentle creature and willing for the animal to feel superior, but prostrating its branches on the ground is against its nature, so it continues to raise them to the sun and air. So the animal, with its claws and teeth, hacks the plant to the ground. Very shortly it realizes that by destroying the plant, it has also destroyed its food supply, and quickly finds itself starving. But the plant grows back from its roots that the animal couldn't reach, in time to keep the animal from dying. When the animal realizes how freely the plant gives of its fruit with no thought of holding back because of what the animal has done to it, the animal hangs its head in shame. "I have only the power to take life," it says to itself. "I can see how little this is compared to the power to give life."

I'm glad I'm human, and would not will to be anything else; but the thought of whether or not we may return as plants and animals has never bothered me. I suppose I'm part Hindu and feel that God is in every living thing. I feel like Tennyson:

Flower in the crannied wall,
I pluck you out of the crannies,
I hold you here, root and all, in my hand,
Little flower—but if I could understand
What you are, root and all, and all in all,
I should know what God and man is.

I don't feel superior to plants and animals. I only feel different from them. Maybe animals have taught me to feel this way. I've had dogs and cats and they were as interesting as I am and had as many powers of their own. They didn't have my powers, and I was in control of them to some extent—not too much—only outwardly, and usually only when they wanted me to be in control.

I have just had a dog die. She was very dear to my wife and me. She was old—sixteen years old is pretty old for a dog. One thing sure, she never felt I was superior. No question in my mind about that. She knew she was superior—a princess. My wife and I were here to wait on her, which was the case. My dogs and cats have all had their own personalities. Just as unique as mine is, just as distinct, just as interesting. I have a feeling, if I got to know—really to know—any creature, no matter how wild, no matter how strange, I'd discover it was just as interesting, just as individual as I am, too.

Something else has taught me that I'm not superior: squirrels. I have a lot of trees in my yard. Squirrels live in them. For a long time, I haven't had a cat. My cat was much more capable of keeping squirrels in their place than I am. I suppose I could shoot them, but I don't want to do that, and anyway, its against the law. These squirrels and I have been fighting a running battle for years now, and so far the squirrels have outwitted me at every turn. It's a terrible thing, to feel that a squirrel is smarter than I am. They sit in the branches of their trees and chatter at me in contempt. I've bought all kinds of bird feeders supposed to keep the squirrels from eating my bird seed. Ha, Ha! They laugh at me as they climb up those squirrel-proof bird feeders or drop down upon them.

I'm a human being who loves sweet corn. I like it more than any other food I've ever tasted. But I only like it fresh. Fresh, it is ambrosia as its sweet buttered kernels pop milky into your mouth. But it turns starchy almost immediately after its picked. You haven't eaten sweet corn unless you've picked it and rushed it to the pot. So I try to grow it in my garden. But the squirrels like sweet corn, too. And they know even better than I when it's at its tastiest, and they get almost every ear. I've tried every device from scarecrows to cayenne pepper, but to no avail. It makes a man weep.

I've often told people, the bravest creature

I've ever met was a little red spider, not an inch long. I met him in my garden. I didn't want to hurt him, he wasn't hurting me, but he was where I wanted to work. So I took a stick to push him out of the way. He attacked me. Not the stick. Me. As is usual with us human beings, I underestimated the intelligence a creature of another species might have. I thought he'd think it was the stick that was attacking him. But he knew it was me, and he finally drove me off.

Oh, I could have stepped on him. But that would have outraged God and nature. He was . . . but what am I saying here, dear girls? Knowing the nature of spiders, I should probably say, *she* was the bravest creature I've ever met. Imagine a creature brave enough to fight for her rights against something so much bigger, as I was. Neither Hercules nor Paul Bunyan, not even Thor, the giant killer, would have dared to stand up against a mountain as gigantic as I must have seemed to that little red spider.

Then there are trees. They are the beautiful culmination of as long a line of evolution as we human beings are. I've always envied them, they have so many qualities I'd like to have.

A tree has found out how
To stay unmoved, yet bow,
And learned as has a hill
The strength of standing still.
The babbling birds and I
With constant shrill outcry
Around the round earth dart
Hoping to find life's heart,
While standing still a tree
Is all it has to be.

I've often said if someone came from a foreign land and told me he had time for only one experience in the United States, I'd tell him to fly to a little town in California named Garberville, rent a car, and drive up the Avenue of the Giants. That's thirty miles of redwoods, and he might add a short drive through Rockefeller Forest that's located at the north end of it. I've done it several times, and I still can't do it without crying. Oh, not because of what we've done to the redwoods, though that's dreadful. No, I cry because of what the redwoods do to me when I'm with them.

These were once the unmatched monarchs of their world. They are almost impervious to fire; the fire can burn off the brush, but the great trees tower high above the fire. They're almost impervious to insects, too. There aren't many birds in a redwood forest because there aren't many bugs there to eat. The redwoods long ago made themselves untasty to bugs. Until we white men came with our steel saws, they could live out their imperturbable and gentle lives for hundreds of years.

I suppose it's just my own imagination, or perhaps it's the way they grow—they grow in clusters—but when I'm among them, I always have a strong sense, I'm not with separate and solitary giants, I'm with creatures that are brooding and protective of one another; they're family creatures; they feel for one another, express affection for one another, communicate with one another.

You see, I don't believe we human creatures are the only ones who can do that. Take dolphins. Most of those who work with them are sure they communicate. There are stories that indicate they may even be protective of human beings. And just because trees don't have nervous systems, don't conclude they can't communicate. I believe intelligence is intelligent enough to find very different means of manifesting itself besides brains and nervous systems, indispensable as these may be to human beings.

I once planted a willow tree, and after it grew, I used to sit beneath its shade and wait for the dryad to step out and speak to me. Finally I realized that wouldn't happen. The tree was waiting for me to learn willow, and I wasn't smart enough to do that. As I say this, I realize I'm not a Hindu, I'm a pagan. I probably am. At least, I have a great deal of admiration and respect for all God's living creatures.

Also, one last thought about transmigration: I've known people who, I've thought, would be happy being certain plants or animals. Do you know what seventeen-year locusts are? Cicadas. For seventeen years the cicada lives on the root of a tree, down under the ground, and all it has to do is suck on the root in the dark. I've had a few friends—I say this sadly—who'd have been happy to have nothing to do for seventeen years except suck on the root of a tree in the dark. And I've known some others who'd be delighted to be house-flies and buzz about annoying everybody.

Before I leave this subject, let me repeat: Unity does not believe in transmigration, in rebirth as plants and animals. I'm not sure there is an official Unity doctrine about the next life because Unity believes as I do that the next life will take care of itself if we take care of this one, and it offers reincarnation simply as a suggestion as to what would be a reasonable way to think it may take place. All the Unity ministers and teachers I know who believe in reincarnation believe we will be reborn as human beings.

However, I feel we need to discuss transmigration because it is a belief held by many millions of persons—by most of the people of Asia as well as by thousands of others, and I want this to be a study of reincarnation in all its ramifications.

Many human beings, especially when they lose a beloved pet, wonder whether animals have a life beyond death. If you can believe that you have, I see no reason why you shouldn't believe that they have, too.

As I consider the geologic record of this planet, with its many fossil remains, I see nothing that would indicate that "That Which Made" the world is a respecter of any special species, human or otherwise. What I see is Life seeking to express itself, Life creating a living world, a world where nothing perishes though all things change. I see a Life

Force so creatively alive that it creates only life, only living creatures, creatures themselves creatively alive. Nowhere do I see creatures completed, but only creatures growing toward completion. I do not know what course life's unfoldment for each and all of us may take before completion is achieved, but I trust with Tennyson ("In Memoriam"):

That nothing walks with aimless feet;
 That not one life shall be destroy'd,
 Or cast as rubbish to the void,
When God hath made the pile complete;

That not a worm is cloven in vain;
 That not a moth with vain desire
 Is shrivell'd in a fruitless fire,
Or but subserves another's gain.

* * * * *

Behold, we know not anything;
 I can but trust that good shall fall
 At last—far off—at last, to all,
And every winter change to spring.

Let me say again, the possibility that I *might* come back as an animal has never entered my mind; but also the possibility that I *might not* come back as an animal has never entered my mind either.

I've never seriously thought about the particular mode of expression my next life may take. If I have thought about it, I imagine I have always assumed I would be human. I believe that is what any human being would probably think.

However, I know that this is a very big world—big beyond imagining—and the creative power of God is creative beyond my imagining, too—and so is His love. So I have no concern as to whether I may be reborn in human or nonhuman form, in this world or another. I'll be me. Or else *I* won't be, in which case I'll have nothing to worry about, will I?

I have come up to here, and wherever I am, whoever I am, whatever I am, I will be what I have come to be. I may not altogether like it, but I have not altogether liked all that I have been and experienced this time.

I have tried to develop such powers and faculties as I have found I had, and I have done my best to use them to make this a joyous and interesting experience for myself and others I have felt responsible for. I believe, whatever world I find myself in, I will accept it and make it my world as I have made this one, and I think you will do this, too. For the world we find ourselves in, whatever it is like, will really be our world, the only world we could be in at that stage of our unfoldment. It will be the world where we can experience what we need to experience, learn what we need to learn, unfold what we need to unfold. It will be the world where you and I can be what you and I have become.

As Brief as a Wink

Everything in nature suggests reincarnation, because everywhere we look, we see a universal theme: recurrence, recurrence, recurrence, recurrence. The world turns as if upon a wheel. Day and night, the seasons, the tides come and go and come once more. The rivers flow into the sea, return as rain, and flow again into the sea. The moon waxes and wanes and waxes again. Everywhere, everywhere we see a principle: recurrence.

Some people seem to find it hard to believe they're going to have another life in another body. I don't see why such a thought seems so hard to accept. We have this life in this body. We did it this time. We don't know how—consciously, that is—but we did it.

Something in our unconscious knew how. It should be easier to believe, having done it once, we might do it again. I believe we've done it many times and surely it must get easier every time.

The thought that I've lived many lives isn't strange to me. How many lives have I lived in this one? How many lives have you lived in this one?

When I was ten, as I told you, I had a complete break in my life. My mother ran away with a man, and took me and a sister with her. We moved fifteen hundred miles, and had an entirely different life in an entirely different kind of environment. There was nobody in it then who had been in it before, except my mother and my sister. Utterly new. I had to build an entirely new life in an entirely new world, with nothing familiar left in it except my mother and my sister.

When I was twenty-one, I came to work at Unity. I lived a different life after that. Unity meant a great change in the things I was doing, in the kind of life I was living, and in the kind of people I was with. Before that I had been with very un-Unity people, and living a very different life. I went to work at Unity, and after that I wasn't at all like the boy who'd been before.

At thirty-one I had a spiritual experience—an intense and passionate illumination—that made such an impression, such a change in me, that I've told people, that was my true birth; I was reborn at that time, through that experience. I was an entirely different person, seeing life from an entirely different viewpoint, and trying to live it in an entirely different way. The thing that shows most clearly how changed I was is my writing. It wasn't at all like the writing I'd done before. From then on I was James Dillet Freeman, writing the poetry and prose I have written ever since, the writing I am writing now.

When I was thirty-five, I lost my first wife, and again I had to form all kinds of new friends and new associations.

At fifty-five I began to travel and to talk for Unity. For twenty years before that I wouldn't talk for Unity. I never went out of Jackson County, Missouri. My wife and I stayed home and worked in our garden. Before that I'd never been in a plane. Since then I've been in more planes than cars. Since then I've been traveling and traveling and talking and talking. In a recent year I made fifteen trips around the United States and to foreign countries. And again it's been a different life from the life I had twenty years ago. Then I couldn't imagine living the life I'm living now.

Now I'm in my seventies and I have retired from more than fifty years' employment at Unity School, and that is making a difference again. I don't yet know what retirement will do to me. I've seen it change a person's life completely, even change the person, almost unrecognizably.

I've lived all these different lives in one lifetime. The life that occurred to me before I was ten had almost no seeable connection with the life lived after that. My life, after I was thirty-one—after I had that spiritual experience—was not in any way like the life I'd lived before, because the man who was living it was not the same man.

Of the people who were an important part of my life when I was ten, none of those people exist today. They're all gone. Of those important at twenty, none of them exist now. Even at thirty, none of them exist now. Not one person who was an important part of my life at those ages is now a part of my life. Not even a particle of my life. Few people important in my life now were there twenty-five years ago. And yet I've lived in one place all the time. I've lived in one place ever since I was ten. Not in one house, but in one community, and I've lived in one house for the last thirty years. I've done one kind of work ever since I was twenty, when I came to work at Unity. Yet I've lived all these very different lives.

The Buddhists have a saying, *Yat sat tat ksanikam*. I like it because it sounds like what it's saying: "Everything is as brief as a wink." *Yat sat tat ksanikam*—how true it is!

Even my body—how many bodies have I had in this life? According to the experts every atom in my body changes every seven or ten years, doesn't it? So every cell, every atom in my body has changed many times. Not one atom of the body I was born with or the body I had, say, at twenty, or thirty, is in me now. My body is composed of an entirely different substance. Not only that, it looks different. Very different. If I could assume the body I had at twenty and the face I had at twenty and the hair I had at twenty, I don't believe anyone I know would recognize me. I would be very surprised if you could. I'd be surprised if I could. I'm not the same person.

On my living room wall I have a picture of

me when I was four years old. My mother gave it to my wife, and she insisted on hanging it there. I was blonde, very blonde, and I was wearing a Buster Brown haircut, combed forward and cut straight across my forehead—I think they called it bobbed—and I had on a Little Lord Fauntleroy suit, with a lace collar and a velvet coat. If that little boy came running up to my closest friend, he wouldn't recognize him. No one in my life today would recognize him.

Life has not let me keep the body I was born with or the one I had at twenty. We've all had—I wonder how many—different bodies in this one lifetime. Why does it seem hard to believe we've had different bodies in other lifetimes?

The world we live in goes through radical changes, too. Kansas City, the city where I've lived since I was ten, is not the city I knew when I was a boy roaming its streets. I live in a suburb now, and when I go into the city, I almost feel lost and I may have to use a map or ask someone how to get where I want to go. Little remains of the city I was raised in—the streets, the highways, the neighborhoods; the stores don't have the same names and they're not in the same places. The highways I drive along were not there; the streets I use to get places are not the same; the neighborhoods are unrecognizably altered. The friends I visit live in parts of the city that weren't even there just a few years ago.

As I said, although I've lived in one city and worked for one organization most of my life, the people in my life now are not the ones who were important in my life at an earlier age, and the work I'm doing is different, too.

Think about yourself. Is this not true of you, too? How many people who are important in your life now were important when you were thirty, or twenty, or ten, or at your birth? Very few, I imagine, even if you have strong family ties. I didn't have those, as I've said.

The point that I'm making here is that the bonds we think tie this life together in a single unified pattern are really not the indissoluble bonds we get to thinking they are. Ties form and ties dissolve. One part of this life may have almost as little coherent connection with another part as another life would have. In certain cases, if we live long enough or suffer certain traumatic experiences, every memory of this life disappears.

We get to thinking people are important to us according to how long they've been part of our lives. And maybe there are people who've been in your life a long time who are important, but some that we've seen every day and been with every day really mean almost nothing to us. There've been a few people who've moved through my life, through forty or fifty years of it, who mean very little to me. I don't mean that in an unpleasant way, they've been pleasant; they've just always been there, on the fringe. On the other hand, there are people with whom I've had brief encounters who have been an extremely important part of my life.

I remember, when I was in college, I remember one date. Oh, I wanted to date that girl! She finally consented to one date. She was going with some other guy. We sat on her sorority porch for a few hours and talked. That's all we did, but she's much more a part of my life than many who have been part of it for years. If you believe in reincarnation, you have to believe that she and I knew each other before we met this time—and I'm looking forward to seeing her again, maybe we can have more than one date sitting on a sorority porch.

As I've said, I've never sought for occult or psychic experiences. I've had a number of them in my life, but I was not seeking them. They came, I feel, because I needed them; they had something to convey to me that was important for me to feel or know. There's no question in my mind that there is a world beyond the world we're usually conscious of, but I see little value in wanting to have experiences in it. I've been around Unity all my life, and I've met a number of unusual people, and I've seen many persons damaged by an overweening interest in occult matters. Such an interest can be a kind of drug addiction. It can separate us from keeping our interest where it must be kept: on the task at hand, on living this life as effectively as we can. I stand with Thoreau: *"One world at at a time, Parker, one world at a time."*

But let me recount an experience I had a few years ago. I had to go to Palm Beach to make some talks. When I arrived, they said, "Jim, we'd like you to visit a nursing home before you leave. They love to have people visit them, and we promised you'll come and read poetry to them." I've done this a number of times. It's a sad and wonderful thing to do. Many of the people don't know whether you're reading poetry or standing on your head, but that's not important. What's important is you're there. You came to be with them. So I'm always glad to go.

But I put off going. Finally it was time for me to go to the airport for my flight home. The man who was taking me said, "The nursing home is on the way to the airport, so you can stop and talk to them." We went and I read the people my poems.

As we were about to leave, a nurse came up to me and said, "Mr. Freeman, there is a patient here who wants to see you. She is terminal, at the point of death, but she feels it's very important that she should see you. Please come and see her."

I said, "Oh, of course."

We walked down a long hall and we walked into her room and there was a woman lying in the bed. I could instantly see that what the nurse had told me was true; the woman was not far from death.

Now, I don't know the woman's name. The nurse told me, of course. But this I knew—the moment I walked into that room—I hadn't really gone to Palm Beach to make those talks I'd made. Oh, I'd made them, of course. But they were merely the means of getting me there. I'd gone to Palm Beach because that woman had called me. I don't know who she was—by name, that is—but I've never met anybody whom I felt a stronger connection with than I felt with that woman, whose name I don't know because it's unimportant what her name is now. Our connection had to have been somewhere else. And it had to have been important. The feeling that surged between us was tremendous. That woman had called me, and I'd answered her call. Of that I have no doubt. Somehow we had had to meet —reestablish our contact—before she went on to another experience. So she'd sent out her call, and I had come. I've always felt that's the only reason—the only real reason—I went down there to Palm Beach.

Time Writes but Time Erases

Something else we should consider before we have gone on so long that we don't have time to consider it is—time. Time. We live in time. We measure our life in terms of time. We experience life in terms of time. If we reincarnate, we reincarnate in time. Often people interested in reincarnation ask how long a time passes between lives. Time is a fascinating substance.

Omar Khayyam has written,

The Moving Finger writes; and having
*   writ,*
Moves on; nor all thy Piety nor Wit
Shall lure it back to cancel half a Line,
Nor all thy Tears wash out a Word of it.

But Omar is not quite right. Time writes,

but time also erases. It's just as much an eraser as it is a pencil.

We get to thinking of the events in life as knots in a long rope, but that's not what life is like at all. When you try to create a mental image of time, you may think it looks like that, but the moment you start to think back through time, you'll see that events aren't arranged in neat chronological order, one after another. They're a jumbled heap. I wrote a little poem about this. I called it "Keepsakes."

After awhile one finds time runs
>*together.*
Did it happen last night, last week,
>*last year, ten*
Years ago, fifty years ago, or when?
After awhile one comes to wonder
>*whether*
It ever happened; some things only seem.
Time is more anesthesia than wings;
And most remarkable of all, the things
That were most real become most like a
>*dream.*
Beginning, ending are not far apart.
A life is not a ribbon to unwind;
The knots one tried to tie in the string of
>*the mind*

Always at last get tangled in the heart.
Life is a drawer of keepsakes—violets,
A faded photograph—one opens the
        drawer
And lifts them out to view, but more and
        more,
Just when they were put in—this one
        forgets.

Dear listener, I don't know how long you have lived. But if you've lived any time at all, you know how true that is. You have your own secret drawer of keepsakes.

Let me say again, time not only writes, time erases. Everyone as he grows older soon realizes how much he is forgetting, even of material he would like to retain. Some people as they grow old forget everything—words and names, skills and knowledge, people and events. The whole of this life passes away from them. I've often wondered, are they preparing for the next life? Only they're preparing for it before they leave this present one.

If we have lived other lives, we don't remember them. Somewhere we've had to put them out of our minds. I've thought perhaps the old who lose their memory just choose to clear their minds here instead of waiting until after they die. I don't offer this as a certainty, but it is an interesting possibility, isn't it? If we've reincarnated, we've all done this forgetting. Where have we done it? Could it be in the womb? Nine months is a very long time with nothing to do except to prepare for birth. I'll return to this thought later.

Most people believe we wipe out the memory of our former life in the interval between death and birth. How long is this interval?

People ask this often, "If we are reborn, how long a time is it between lives?" Cora Fillmore—she was Charles Fillmore's second wife—once asked me this. I answered her by asking her, "What did Charles say?" She said, "He never said."

Since then I've heard a number of lecturers lecture on reincarnation and some of the lecturers have been completely willing to tell their listeners exactly how long the interval between lives is. The only trouble is, different lecturers seem to have different ideas. Some say it's a short time; others say it's eons.

It's interesting that in Dr. Stevenson's studies of those who say they remember a past incarnation—the only scientific studies of reincarnation I know of—in most cases the time that had passed between their former life and their present one was very short. However, it's a subject about which, considering our present knowledge, I don't think it's possible to come up with an exact answer, and I try to be cautious in coming up with exact answers when I don't have any. But in this case, I have given it a great deal of thought, and I have come up with an unusual thought about it.

I'm not sure there is any time in between lives. Let me say that again. I'm not sure there is any time in between lives.

Think about time. Perhaps the only meaning time has is in relation to us in this three-dimensional world we live in. There is much in modern science that would indicate this might be so. Scientists have made time relative; they relate it to speed; they limit it by the speed of light; they tie it to space and call it space-time.

Immanuel Kant held that the mind is structured to think in terms of time and space. Time and space are the sine qua non of our physical world, that without which there is none. They are the basic stuff from which this world of things and thoughts in which we now have our existence is constructed. It's impossible for us to think except in terms of time and space; but inversely, just as time and space are necessary in order for us to conceive of the physical world, so it may also be that the physical world is necessary for us to conceive of time and space. In any other mode of existence there may not be time, at least as we think of time.

One thing I am sure about time—it's not the tick-tock sort of thing we get to thinking it is. We human beings seem almost obsessed by the need to know what time it is. Most animals seem content to know it's morning when the light comes on and evening when it goes out—and they have a sense of the passing of the seasons. They know when it's time to eat and time to sleep—time to nest and time to leave the nest. And they seem content with that. Not we human beings. From sundials to cesium atom clocks—we seem to have a strident need to know exactly what time it is, to the second, and in our time, even to the eleven-millionth of a second.

I've always liked the story Charles Fillmore used to tell. He'd say he didn't care when people looked at their watches while he was speaking, but it did bother him when they raised them to their ears to see whether or not they were running. After listening to me this long, I imagine you may be doing that.

Most of us carry watches and we have a compulsion to keep them right to the second, as if the time given by our watches were some sort of an absolute that life measures itself by. When daylight saving time was proposed, people opposed it, saying we were interfering with God's time. I have a feeling, God doesn't have any time. He has eternity.

The tick-tock time we keep with our watches is just the yardstick we've invented for our convenience. It's strange that we should think of it as God's time because almost nothing in God's world goes by it except us. Hardly anything in the world moves at the fixed, unchanging pace our tick-tock time seems to suggest is the way of things. Scientists have had to invent solar time, which is what the sun moves to, and sidereal time, which is what the stars move to.

I think some of us somehow have come to feel the standard time we keep with our watches—that is, when we're not violating God's time by turning them to daylight saving—has been here throughout eternity.

279

Standard time is only 100 years old. We invented it because we'd invented railroads and people had to agree on what time it was in order to make train connections. Before that, each railroad had its own time, every jeweler had a clock in his window, and if you set your watch by it, that was the right time for you.

To see how different ideas of time can be, consider the Eastern notion of time. We in the West usually think of time as an arrow shot through space or as a river running along its course, because we think we're going somewhere. The Hindus do not have this notion, they have such a sense of cycle and recurrence. Life is a process of recurrence, they teach, of things happening over and over and over. So when a Hindu tries to describe time, he thinks of it as a pool, a still pool, and into the center of the pool he drops a pebble, and a ripple runs out to the edge of the pool and runs back on itself—and that's time. A very different notion, as you can see.

Time is relative. If time is important to you, you might like what the Hindus do to it. For the Hindus have a fantastic sense of its vastness. They figure time in mahayugas, 4,320,000 years. But that's only the beginning. One thousand mahayugas make one kalpa, one day in the life of a Brahma. The day of a Brahma is followed by a night of equal length, when all the worlds and all the beings contained in them disappear. A Brahma lives for 311,040,000,000,000 human years. Then everything returns into the void for an equal period before the whole process starts over again. The gods are hardly ever in a hurry.

The Hindus make even the gods mortal, but some of them do survive for a long while. They tell a beautiful story about the god, Indra. When Indra slew the dragon that was destroying the earth, and restored the earth to life, he felt very important. So he summoned the god of arts and crafts, Vishvakarman, and ordered him to erect the most magnificent palace that had ever been erected. But no matter what Vishvakarman erected, Indra wanted something more palatial yet, and he gave the divine craftsman no rest. Finally Vishvakarman went to Vishnu, the highest god, and asked for help. The next day a beautiful and saintly boy appeared in the palace of Indra. The boy began to lecture Indra on the vastness of time and the relative mortality of gods like Indra. As he spoke, a procession of ants appeared in the hall, in a column four yards wide, and they paraded across the floor. As the boy watched them, he began to laugh. "Why are you laughing?" Indra asked. "Oh, Indra," said the boy, "each of these ants was once an Indra."

The greatest symbol of the Orient is the wheel. I, too, think it's a wonderful symbol but only if you think of it as moving rather than stationary. That makes time recurring, repeating the pattern as it turns, but never the same, never returning to the same spot. That makes time not a circle, but a spiral, and a spiral is a living form. It's not fixed. It moves. It circles outward and upward. It's interesting, isn't it? Scientists have identified the DNA molecule, the basic substance of which all life on earth is formed, as a spiral. Also, the usual form of a galaxy is spiral, and we call them spiral nebulas. We happen to live in one, the Milky Way. Unlike a spinning wheel, a spiral is a pattern of growth.

As I say, time is relative. It's elastic, it's rubbery. If you think about it for a few minutes, you'll feel how rubbery it is. If I told you I'm not going to say anything for one minute—in my case, I've been talking so long, you'd probably say, "Thank God." But if I actually didn't say anything for a minute and just stood silent, you'd feel the minute was endless.

You know how true this is any time when you have to wait. Waiting is the easiest—and oh, the hardest—way to stretch time out, to slow time down, to elongate the time interval. Have to wait—with nothing to do except wait for five minutes, ten minutes, twenty minutes—and the minutes aren't minutes, they're hours. It can't take that long for a few minutes to pass! You keep looking at your watch in disbelief.

You've had the opposite experience, too. You're working at something in which you're totally absorbed, and suddenly you look up and exclaim, "Where did the time go!" Time melts away and is almost as if it were not there when we're absorbed in something that leaves no thought for anything else. I've had this happen when I'm writing, especially when I'm writing at my best and words are pouring out of me. Hours and hours may go by, and I have no sense of time passing.

That's an interesting reflection on time. The more our minds are on ourselves, the more we have nothing to take them off ourselves, as when we're just waiting, the more real time becomes. We become aware of it, every elongated second of it. But when we lose ourselves in something more than ourselves, time disappears.

Could our sense of time somehow be connected with our sense of self? Is time the medium in which self abides? The more conscious of self we are, the more conscious of time we are. And usually the more conscious of time we are, the more wearisome life becomes. We say of a man in jail, he has to "do time." When we view ourselves in terms of time, do we all feel like prisoners?

When we see things from the aspect of selflessness—and isn't that another name for love?—do we see them from the aspect of eternity? Is this what the great religions—or if not the religions, at least their founders—are trying to teach us? As we lose our sense of self, we find our meaning not in the ebb and flow, the transitoriness of time, but the abiding reality, the timelessness of eternity. I've always thought that heaven is the way things look when we look with eyes of love. I've always thought that's the way Jesus looked at everything—with eyes of love. That's why the things He looked at changed—and the people He looked at changed, too: they found health and peace and joy and new meaning in life.

That has to be the way God looks at us, with eyes of love and from the aspect of eternity. That's why sometimes from behind the scenes, where we play out the little roles we seem appointed to play in this act of our lives—sometimes from behind the scenes, I hear gentle laughter that I've always felt was God's. He knows that whatever we do to ourselves and one another, underneath are the everlasting arms, and they are love's. In terms of the eternal drama, which is His immortal composition (this present act is just a passing fragment) all is well.

But I don't have time for eternity, though you may be thinking that's what I'm taking. Let's get back to time.

If you want to see how relative time is, how variable it may be, think about your dreams, and about the length of time in dreams. I'm not sure that time even occurs in a dream, at least sequentially, with one thing coming after another, as we ordinarily view it. When I look back on the jumble of some of my dreams, a hodgepodge of utterly unrelated and uncompleted happenings, popping time-wise and space-wise in and out of one another,

I have wondered if it may not be, at least in some dreams, that events occur all at one time, or at least with no relation to our ordinary conception of time. We put them in sequential order when we awake, because that's the way our waking minds are programmed, to arrange everything in time. We see time as a procession of consecutive moments, each one the same length as another, each one following another in orderly, foreordained fashion. Time is laid out in our minds much the way space is, except that it is measured in minutes instead of yards. Modern science is beginning to question if either time or space is this kind of fixed continuum.

A friend of mine told me that once he was driving a car and ahead of him, much less than 100 yards down the road, he saw a bridge two or three seconds away at the speed he was driving. At that moment he fell asleep at the wheel. He then dreamed a dream in which he did many things that took a great deal of time, and he woke up and had not yet reached the bridge. Fortunately for him!

We really don't know too much about our dreams because in order to interpret them, we have to put them in terms our awakened mind can deal with. I have a feeling that time is a very different thing when we dream.

In deep sleep, dreamless slumber, is there any sense of time at all? When we awaken from deep sleep, we often have to look at the clock to know how much time has passed. Sometimes we think, "Oh, it has to be morning." But when we look at the clock we find we've slept only one hour. At other times we are asleep until morning, but when we first wake, we think, "I've just fallen asleep; I've only slept for a few minutes."

When I sleep deeply and well, the sun's usually up when I awaken. That's how I know it's morning. When people enter into comas where they sleep for many years, I wonder if they have any sense of the passage of time. Remember Rip Van Winkle, who slept for twenty years? I don't believe he would have had any idea how old he was when he awakened. At least not until he looked at his beard! With all of us, if we should sleep for a long time, except that we could see whether or not our hair and our fingernails had grown, we'd have no idea whether we'd slept for a long time or a short time.

Another thing that shows how variable time is—scientists speak of physiological time. Our physiological time interval varies;

as we grow older, time speeds up for us. We don't need scientists to tell us that, if we are older. We're aware of it. Someone has said, old age is the time when the hours grow longer and the years grow shorter. Time moves faster and faster the longer we live. Scientists tell us that we have this sense of time speeding up because our body functions slowly slow down. As we take longer to do what once we did quickly, we have the sense of time hurrying by us. By treating us with microwave therapy or certain drugs, scientists can warm us up for a little while so that time will move more slowly for us again.

Apparently we've always known there is a connection between body warmth and our time interval. There's a great story in the Bible. "Now King David was old and he could not get warm. So his servants said, 'Let a young maiden be sought for my Lord, the King, and let her lie in his bosom that my Lord, the King, may be warm.'" His servants were hoping to give the old king a little more time—and I guess a little more life during that time.

Time runs slow and is long when we're young. Part of feeling young is feeling we have all the time in the world to do the least thing in. Watch a child; he has forever, and he has it now. Time is short and races by when we grow old. Part of feeling old is feeling time is running out on us.

Considering this physiological fact, that time speeds up as we grow older, I've wondered about the nine months we spend in our mother's womb—how long, in psychological terms, in terms of our mental life span from conception to death, how long would this period in the womb be? We don't know, of course, because we have no memories of the time we spent in the womb, and even if we could remember what life there was like, we'd have no way to compare the time interval between conception and birth with the time interval between birth and death, because the physiological time interval is a constant variable. At seven it's many times longer than at seventy, and at our seventh month in the womb how much longer is each moment than when we're seven years old? And at the seventh day of conception, how much longer than at the seventh month?

All one can do is wonder, but it is possible that the nine months in the womb may be as long as, say, nineteen years spent out of it, or maybe even ninety? I've wondered, could it be that the womb is the other side of the tomb?

From the standpoint of divine justice, this would make a great deal of sense, for it would make us truly accountable for the world we inherit. The world we would be reborn in would be the world as we had left it nine months before. If we'd sown the wind, it would be we who reaped the whirlwind. Fair, no?

People have given all kinds of descriptions of what life in the next world, the spirit world, is like. If you believe in reincarnation, this would be the time between death and rebirth.

Poets like Dante have usually made heaven and hell very material places where very flesh-and-blood spirits enjoy very physical pleasures and suffer very physical pains. But I think most intelligent people realize these can't be realistic. When we die, we no longer have bodies, so our experiences, whatever they may be, will necessarily have to be those that spirits may experience.

Both ancients and moderns, when they try to describe this world in spirit-like terms, have usually not been able to make it more than a nebulous, insubstantial affair, in which our spirits float amorphously and ectoplasmically about.

If we might have any memories, even the most indistinct memories of our nine months in the womb, mightn't we describe them much like this? For nine months, months where perhaps our time interval is fantastically extended, we have only to rest in the sealed bubble of the placenta and prepare for birth.

If you believe in reincarnation, consider, would that not be an ideal place? From our adult point of view, nine months seems short. But considered in the light of time's variability, who knows? Perhaps it even varies from person to person.

Somewhere between reincarnations, we have to erase the memory of our past one, for we are born—all of us—as if we began anew, our mind a clean slate. A *tabula rasa*, that's the way the great English philosopher, John Locke, described the mind. He said that at birth the mind is a *tabula rasa*, a clean slate. I don't think we are quite a clean slate. We're more a pattern of instincts, tendencies, powers, and potential. Indeed, each of us starts out with an extremely complex genetic arrangement that differentiates us from all other creatures. But clean slate we are as far as conscious memories of a former life.

This has nothing to do with reincarnation, but John Locke's notion of a *tabula rasa* has had a profound effect on all of us politically. Most of the Founding Fathers of the Republic were students of his philosophy, and when Jefferson wrote the Declaration of Independence, it was from the notion of *tabula rasa*, he took his great phrase, *all men are created equal.*

In the warm sea of the womb, in a state of physical suspension, almost immobile—oh, our mothers complain, we can kick—with every need taken care of, with body and mind almost totally shut off from contact with the outer world—what better place could we find ourselves in, to review and release the memories of the last life so that we can begin our new life clean of any hindrances?

As I say, I don't offer this notion as a fact, but as an interesting suggestion. It is, isn't it?

As to the time it takes to reincarnate, it is as it is with many things connected with this subject: no one can make exact computations. It would be reasonable to suppose that it would vary from individual to individual.

The time between incarnations may depend

on how anxious we are to be on our way again, or what our needs are. What are the drives in our soul?

Let's look at how we are doing this time. It may throw some light on the side of life we cannot see. The hidden side of the moon, when the astronauts reached there, turned out to be much like the side we see from earth.

Some of us were born squawling and kicking into this life and have protested furiously almost every foot of the way. Some stay for a very short time; others come eager to accept the challenge and adventure. They live for many years as fully and energetically as they can.

It would seem to me that the time between times, like the present time, will take care of itself. It will depend on consciousness. The same is true as to the same or another place and form—whether we will return here on earth, and will have human form, or whether we will experience life in some very different mode of manifestation.

I have never seen why these matters should overly concern us. The place, the form, the time will take care of themselves, and they will be right. We are immortal beings and we draw our own life to us.

We will be we, and we will draw to us the life we have come up to. Isn't that the only way it can be, and isn't that what we want?

For years I have kept a little piece of writing in my files. I don't know who wrote it. I don't think I did, though I'm not sure I didn't. I wish I had, because it expresses how I feel about this whole matter.

Maybe in another universe matter will be equally illusory but on a different plane. Instead of seeing a rose in Arabella's hair, one will see a heart-thrill with dimensions and surfaces. It will be possible to bark your shins on an anxiety lying loose on the stairs in the dark, and fears will be extracted with corkscrews.

Shall We Meet Again?

Another reason people reject the idea of reincarnation—and its an understandable one—is that they hope to have those dear to them in this life back with them in the next, and they think reincarnation rules out this possibility. I know how they feel. I want to meet those I've loved. There are a few people I've prayed with all my heart to meet again. But I believe we will.

Believing in reincarnation doesn't prevent me from believing we meet our loved ones. On the contrary. Because we may reincarnate, there's a possibility we may meet over and over as we work out our individualities. I think many of us have shared life before this one. I think that's often the reason we were drawn to people this time around; we loved them in past lives—or wanted to. It seems to me, reincarnation is the only belief that gives us any reasonable hope that there's a possibility of meeting dear ones.

The question to me is not, Do we meet our dear ones? But, How do we meet them? How can we meet them?

I think the way most people imagine they're going to meet their dear ones in the next world defies imagination when you think it through. When you look at it with even a touch of realism, you see how impossible it is.

Let's take the common picture many religious groups draw. You die and cross the river Jordan or the river Styx, or you enter the next world. Usually the religions that paint this picture have their members going up to heaven, although it would seem to me that by their theology there's a horrible chance that the trip would be in the other direction. Anyway, as you step off Charon's ferry, there are all of your friends and relatives who have gone before you, waiting on the bank to greet you.

But let's look at this picture. Is the you who steps off Charon's boat, the you who died? Do you look like the person who is laid out at the funeral home? If you do, will the relatives who passed on when you were a child know who you are? And the relatives waiting for you, will they look like they did when you last saw them—the children like children and the old folks like old folks? The moment you examine this picture you see that it loses all perspective. Who's gonna meet whom?

We are separated from friends for a few years, and we may change so much we don't know one another when we meet. I was separated from my father for twelve years, and we passed one another on the street and did not recognize one another.

There are a number of people I would like very much to meet again. Let me talk for a moment about just one of these who was very important to me—my grandfather—and let's try to imagine what a reunion between us in the next life would be like. As I said, he was very dear to me when I was a little boy. We never saw each other after I was ten, because my mother ran away and took me with her.

And before we go further, let's look at my mother's running away in the way she did it—she broke up our family in an especially unpleasant way, guaranteed to create unhappiness for almost everyone concerned. It's not improbable that part of the reason my mother did what she did was to hurt my grandfather.

Looking back, not from a boy's, but from an adult's viewpoint, I have the feeling there was a great deal of ambivalence in my mother's attitude toward my grandfather. I've come to believe most close relationships, if they last long enough, are hardly ever pure love affairs. The more we have to do with someone else, the more we may be drawn to him, but also the more we may have to be angry with him about.

My mother's relationship with my grandfather—and such ambivalent relationships are more the rule than the exception—has to make us wonder, doesn't it? Just how eternal will these eternal relationships that are going to last from life to life be? Think about some of the relationships in your own life.

From bits of information my mother let drop through the years, I think my grandfather was a tyrant with his family. I remember my lovely little grandmother almost as a shadow, and I think that's all she'd been in his presence. He'd lost all his sons—four of them—to childhood diseases, so he'd tried to make my mother into a boy. But my mother was just as smart and strong-willed as he was. She showed him how female a female can be.

My mother knew how dear I was to my macho grandfather. I was the four boys he'd lost. Maybe that's why she took me with her when she ran.

Oh, my grandfather was a tyrant with me, too, but if I resented him, I loved him so much I didn't let myself know I resented him. He had me walking before I should have, and it wasn't enough to have me tottering around on my feet when I should have still been crawling on hands and knees, to make sure I'd grow up to be the macho boy he wanted, he had me lugging a Civil War cannonball. A history of the Civil War, full of bloody battle pictures, was one of the first books I read. My grandfather had been a boy in the Civil War. He'd lost eight uncles in it, and he damned the South and the Democratic Party. My grandfather was an unusually strong man physically, and also a man of strong opinions and emotions. Once, a barber gave me a crewcut in November. When my grandfather saw me, he loaded his gun and started out toward the barbershop. A barber stupid enough to cut all the hair off a boy in the winter should not be allowed to do it to another one, he thought. Fortunately, my grandmother was able to call and warn the barber to get out of the shop before my grandfather got there.

My grandfather had been raised on a farm and probably had had very little education, but he knew the value of one. He made me learn the alphabet before I could talk. He was ingenious. He would speak the letter, and I would have to point it out on a chart.

He taught me to read and write when I was three, and the books he taught me to read from were the Bible and the "Red Fairy Book." I can't recommend them as teaching aids for little children. They both left me scared white. The "Red Fairy Book" was full of pictures of ogres and giants and trolls and witches, usually in the act of dispatching helpless human beings. My grandfather not only believed in witches, he'd known a few, he'd even shot at one or two, but he hadn't had a silver bullet in his gun, and you have to have a silver bullet to shoot a witch. You can see why I slept with a rubber dagger and a hammer under my pillow. He had me read books about the Norse gods, too, and naturally Thor was my hero. He was the giant killer, and I think there were a few giants in my childhood I would have liked to use his hammer on.

Oh, he taught me to read poetry, too. I was brought up on Edgar Allan Poe. He's almost as scary as the Bible and the "Red Fairy Book." My grandfather lured me into memorizing Poe's poems. Then he'd give me a penny to recite them for his friends.

I'm left-handed, but because he wasn't going to have a left-handed grandson, I write with my right hand—illegibly, of course.

Although he was short, he was immensely strong, and in his youth had been a rough-and-tumble fighter. He taught me to fight—I was never any good—and to swear like a trooper—I've been too good at that. He was a hunter and a champion trapshooter. By the time I was six, he had me out dragging a gun through the snow after him. I still have his old shotgun; he left it to me.

I would have done anything for him. I loved him. I adored him. And I'd like to think I'll meet him again. But am I going to be a little boy of, say, eight or nine? Is he going to be a man of sixty or seventy, or whatever he was?

Would he be willing to be that old man? One thing sure, I'm not willing to spend eternity as a little boy. I'm not willing to go back and be a ten-year-old, however much he might like it. I don't think he'd be willing either. He was a very vital, physical man, proud of his strength and athletic prowess. I don't think he'd be willing to settle for old age.

Then there's my grandmother, his wife. You have to bring her into the picture. I'm certain she wouldn't want him to be that old man of sixty or seventy. Maybe, of course, she wouldn't want him at all. But if she did, she'd want the young lover she had had— who'd wooed her and won her, and taken her off to be his beloved wife.

If my grandfather and I are going to meet again—and I hope we will—it won't be as an old man and a little boy. There is only one way we could meet—it will be as we have come to be. I was a little boy and he was an old man this time. The next time he'll be what he becomes, and I'll be what I become, and each of us will accept himself and be drawn toward the other as each of us has come to be, just as it was this time—or maybe we won't. That's the only way it could be.

Our present life shows us what the pattern

must be, doesn't it? We grow toward people and we grow away from them, right here. All kinds of people have moved into our lives and out of them. They're here for a while, then they're gone. Maybe they move away to a different city, or maybe they just move away in consciousness and become interested in a different kind of life. Or we become interested in a different kind of life, and we move away.

I have a grandson, as I told you. When he was five, I was crazy about that boy. We were very close. He's twenty now, and the relationship has changed. I still love him, but not in the same way. He probably loves me in the same way I now love him—as a member of the family. He has no interest in me. Why should he? He's worrying about what he's going to make of his life. If he has a strong interest in anything, it's girls! I don't blame him. If I should meet my grandson in the next life, naturally I hope he'd be more like five than twenty. But when you stop and think about it, the whole notion of his being five or twenty is preposterous. He's going to be whatever he meanwhile grows to be—in the time that passes before we meet. And so am I. In this life and any other.

Interestingly, the people from whom we

got this notion of meeting again in the next life, the Zoroastrians—they tried to give it at least an element of reason, by saying, if you die as an adult, in the next life you'll always be forty years old. If you die as a child, you'll always be fifteen. They thought that made it make some sense, and it is better than what we Christians have come up with. But it still isn't very sensible. Would you want to be forty forever? Or if you were a child, would you want to be fifteen forever? I don't believe it. I don't think that's what you'd want to be at all. You'd want to grow. You have to grow. Life made you to grow.

I saw an interesting statistic that shows how preposterous is this notion of our getting together with our dear ones. We want to be with our parents. But they want to be with their parents; and their parents want to be with their parents. By the time you get twenty generations down the line, each one wanting to be with the others whom they love, you'd have 1,048,576 people getting together for life in the next world. That's more like a traffic jam than a get-together. I wonder how heavenly it would be!

The reason it doesn't make sense is that we can't stop life, and that's what we'd have to do—stop life! There are some interesting myths about the gods trying to hold life at the point they've wanted it to be. The goddess of dawn, Aurora, fell in love with a Greek, Tithonus, and made him immortal. But she could not stop life, and at last, out of pity, because of the miserable creature he became, she changed him into a grasshopper.

The Japanese tell the story of Izanagi and Izanani. They were lovers, and mighty ones. Out of their union they produced the islands of Japan. But Izanani died in childbirth, bringing forth the fire god. She warned Izanagi not to follow her, but he pursued her into the ghastly, ghostly underworld of Yomi, the land of the dead, hoping to bring her back. When he lit a torch, he saw her as she had become in death's decay. He had to run back to the world of the living, pursued by the angry, humiliated Izanani and the hideous females of Yomi, and he barely made it, to bar the gates of death so no one else could try his foolish and futile stunt.

The greatest of all stories dealing with the theme that you can't bring life to a halt is Goethe's *Faust*. It is universally considered to be one of the world's great masterpieces. The play revolves around the contract the magician Faust makes with the Devil, Mephistopheles. Mephistopheles tells Faust that he will give him anything he asks for, with the provision that Faust's soul will belong to him, the Devil, whenever Faust says that what he has is so satisfying he'd like to stop right there and stay at that point forever. *Faust* is a great piece of literature because it states this great truth: You can't stop. You can't stop life. You can't stay at one point forever. The moment you do, you are in thrall to the forces of darkness and dissolution, you begin to stagnate, to disintegrate. There is no standing still. You're going forward or slipping back. When we quit running, we start rusting. When we quit growing, we start rotting.

If there's one great truth about life, it is this: Life is change. I've written a piece about this:

As we live, we all move from level to level in consciousness. We go up a path, and as we go, things change and we change. . . . It is as when we move from city to city. We can never go back. We may think we can go back. We may wish to go back. We may look back with longing and think to ourselves, "Ah, that was

*the good life then!" We may even go back
to what we thought was the city we left.
But it will never be there, not the city we
remember. Once you come up a step, you
can never go back. When you start to go
back, you quickly find that you can't
warm yourself by last night's fire, however brightly it may blaze in your
memory. Now it's only a heap of ashes,
and if you would be warm, you must
build another fire. . . . Once you have run
with the foxes, how can you go back to
being a hare again? Better to be the least
of foxes than king of the hares. . . . All the
happy toys of childhood—the dolls and
the lead soldiers—where are they now?*

Life never stands still. Life is to be lived.
It is to be lived at the level we've come up to.
We can't hold on to anything for long. If we
do, we'll wish we'd let it go. We can't even
hold on to a breath; we have to let it go in
order to breathe again.

Isn't this what the Master, Jesus, is telling us in His parable of the talents? The third
servant tried to hold on to the talent the
master had given him by burying it. The
master took even his one talent away and
threw him out of doors.

Life is to be lived—this life and any other. This is just as true in the hereafter as in the here. To find life's meaning we have to let go what has been and have faith in the ever-renewing now. I'd like to read a story I wrote about life and death and the hereafter. It's in my book, *Of Time and Eternity*. It's about a little monk.

Once there was a little saint who had lived a long and holy and happy life, so one day God sent His angel to bring him to the abode of eternity. The angel found the little saint in the kitchen, washing the pots and pans.

"The time has come," said the angel, "for you to take up your abode in eternity. God has sent me to bring you to Him."

"I thank God for thinking of me," said the little saint, "but as you can see, there is this great heap of pots and pans to be washed as well as quite a few other things that need doing to set this kitchen in order. I don't want to seem ungrateful, but do you think I might put off taking up my abode in eternity until I have finished this?"

The angel looked at him in the wise and

loving way of angels. "I'll see what can be arranged," he said and vanished.

The little saint went on with his pots and pans and the few other things that needed doing in the kitchen and a great number of other things besides that.

One day as he stood hoeing in the garden, there again was the angel. The saint shrugged his shoulders as if to say, "I am sorry about this," and pointed with his hoe up and down the garden rows.

"Look at all these weeds," he said. "You can see for yourself all the things that need to be done in this garden. There are corn and beans to be planted and a row of marigolds along the fence there, and the cold frame needs to be rebuilt. Do you think eternity can hold off a little longer?"

The angel looked at the saint and smiled and again he vanished.

So the saint went on hoeing the garden, and after he had hoed the garden he painted the barn, and after he had painted the barn, he had the poor to visit.

What with one thing and another, time raced ahead until one day he was in the

hospital tending the sick. He had just fin-
ished giving a drink of cold water to a
feverish patient when he looked up and
there was the angel once more.

This time the saint said nothing. He
just spread his hands in a gesture of res-
ignation and compassion and drew the
angel's eyes after his own around the
hospital ward where all the many suf-
ferers were waiting for him to tend to
them. Without a word the angel van-
ished.

That evening when the little saint went
back to the monastery, he ate his simple
meal with his fellow monks and after-
wards sat for a while with a couple of his
cronies swapping stories. But when he
had gone to his cell and sunk down on his
pallet, he began to think about the angel
and how he had put him off for such a
long time. It had been a very busy day
and suddenly he felt very old and very
tired, and he said, "God, if You would
like to send Your angel again, I think I
would like to see him now."

He had no sooner spoken than the
angel stood beside him.

"If you still want to take me," said the

saint, "I am ready to go with you now to take up my abode in eternity."

The angel looked at the little saint in the wise and loving way angels look and he smiled a warm, soft smile. "Where do you think you have been?" he said.

Perfect, but Not Perfected

Charles Fillmore, who founded Unity, thought you were meant to live forever in this body, here on this earth. He thought if you didn't make it this time, you'd be brought back to try again. He very much wanted to make it this time. He tried, and he did a good job of it for ninety-four years, considering that he'd been given up to die when he was ten. He helped a lot of other people to live, too. Personally, I'm glad he made the effort. And personally, I agree with what he taught. I think we should be able to live forever. I don't believe God made us to suffer and die. He made us in His image, so He must have made us perfect. I have to believe God made me perfect, or I have to believe He's not a perfect God. But being made perfect doesn't mean we were made perfected. Part of our perfection as living creatures is that we're not perfected. We're alive and growing! Life is perfect, but not perfected. There's a tremendous and important difference. I think I've said before in these talks that only when caterpillars are caterpillars will butterflies be butterflies. The perfect butterfly is, for a time, a caterpillar; and it's no less perfect when it's a caterpillar than when it's a butterfly.

Life's a journey but the journey isn't over— it's only begun. Suppose God said to you, "I'm going to give you a trip around the world." And you said, "Thank You, God." He said, "How did you like it?" You said, "But I haven't yet even begun." He said, "Oh, yes, I gave you the trip complete and completed. Look back and you'll see what a perfect trip it was. You've had an absolutely perfect trip around the world." I think you would feel you'd been tricked, not tripped. I think you'd feel you'd never had a trip. The joy of a journey is not in having arrived. The joy is in the journeying. To be perfect is not being perfected. It's to be moving in the direction you're meant to be moving in. I happen to think that's a divine direction.

Which would you rather be, Michelangelo's David, flawless in the square at Florence, or a newborn child? Earlier in the lectures, I read you Chuang tze's charming thought about life and dreaming. Let me tell you a story about him.

One day when he was fishing, an official approached him and asked him to become a state administrator. Chuang just kept on fishing.

Finally he said, "I've heard that in the city there's a sacred tortoise which has been dead some three thousand years. The prince keeps him perfectly preserved in a beautiful chest on the temple altar. Now, what do you think? Would this tortoise rather be dead and venerated, or would it rather be alive and wagging its tail in the mud?"

"Why, of course, it would rather be alive," said the official.

"Begone, then," said Chuang tze, "I, too, will wag my tail in the mud."

I think God made us to live forever, but at the level I've come up to, I'm glad we don't, because I'm not ready for eternal life. Even if an angel came down and said, "Jim, I'm going to give you two hundred more years of life," do you know how I'd feel? I'd feel scared. I'd think, "How am I going to stay alive, really alive, and happy, for two hundred more years?" I'm having problems at seventy. I had problems at seventeen, too, and I survived them, and heaven knows, I have so much growing to do, I'm sure it would take me much more than two hundred years to make it. But the thought that I would have to do it here, in this present shape and form, in these present conditions of life, with my present limitations, would be a frightening prospect. I don't want to keep on living unless I can keep on being alive. It is not only myths that point out what a dreary business it is to be kept existing in this body and not stay alive. All around us we see miserable people who are doing it. I do not want to be another Tithonus.

So if I were suddenly confronted with two hundred more years, I'd tell the angel, "All right, all right, I accept it, but first, will you give me a mild dose of amnesia?" It's interesting that that's what I think I'd ask for. If we reincarnate, that's what we get.

If that prayer were not granted, I would pray for the courage to quit doing most of the things I'm now doing and head back to college and try to master entirely new fields of knowledge that would force me to seek a new outlook and begin again. Is there any question as to what my great need would be if I had any hope of keeping my sanity and my health? I would need to start afresh. And if I just kept on being and doing what I am now being and doing, I doubt if I'd have the strength of character to make voluntarily the changes I'd need to make. Habit is a comfortable companion.

You may be asking, wouldn't this fellow want to keep on writing his poetry and keep on seeking the spiritual growth and unfoldment he talks about?

As to spiritual growth and unfoldment, it is because I value it so highly that I would feel such need to gain and maintain a fresh and alive outlook, for that is the essence of spiritual growth and unfoldment.

As to my writing, I am sure that sooner or later I would be back at it; a creative life is the only life worth living. But if there is anything a writer knows, it is that in order to keep his writing at its best, he needs to keep the creative juices of his spirit flowing at a very high intensity, and to do that, he needs to constantly renew his inspiration and to have unflagging energy.

I don't know what diminishes—whether it is incentive or energy or originality or what— but clearly some vital spark sooner or later goes out. You have only to look at the works of famous writers and artists and scientists to see that, if they work long enough, though their creativity may expand for a time, sooner or later inventiveness and inspiration fade and the work becomes largely humdrum and repetitive. "Shades of the prison house begin to close." I don't want this to happen to me.

To stay alive you have to stay flexible and self-renewing. You have to keep on growing. As I have often said, I envy trees, because when they stop growing, they're dead. Unfortunately, it's not always that way with us human beings. Few if any of us grow more receptive to change with the changing years. Habits of thought bind us more tightly round, and cause us to cling to attitudes and behavior patterns we long to be free of.

This is why I pray that my belief in reincarnation will turn out to be true. One lifetime is not enough. I see too much to learn for me to hope to learn it in a single life. I know how far I fall short of what I want to be, of what God created me to become.

I am afraid I have run about as far as I can run in the race I am running now. Do not misjudge me. I shall run as long as I can run, and I shall run with all my heart and all my mind and all my might. But I feel a tightening and stiffening, not only in my limbs but in the sinews of my soul, and I think I will run a better race if I can rest awhile and renew my strength before I have to run anew.

At the level where we human beings have arrived, I believe death is a kindness. All you have to do is look around at the old in our society to see how great a kindness it is. Someday we human beings may grow spiritually to the place where we're alive enough, and that means flexible enough, open enough to change, that we can keep on living forever without having to die in order to be renewed. We may grow to the place where we learn how to free ourselves from the bonds of habit, the fixed limitations in which we encase ourselves now. When we do that, perhaps we will live forever. But as for now, I think, death is a kindness. Some day we'll know why we die, and when we know all the reasons, we'll see death as a natural part of life—an incident as birth is—an incident and not a cruel and needless anguish. Not anguish at all to the dying, only to the living. The death of someone we love is anguish to those of us who survive because we're afraid of death. We're afraid of it because it's the unknown. We're afraid that perhaps our loved one has suffered extinction or is in some kind of strange pain. Also, our anguish is for ourselves. We've suffered a loss. As of now, death is a necessary kindness, our having come no further than we've come. It's as kind as sleep, as darkness, as winter, as stillness.

Out of His infinite mercy God has made the day and the night, and divided them with sleep. Eternity might overwhelm us, and I think it would, if we had to face or comprehend it all at once. But we can face it and we can comprehend it, one day at a time, one life at a time. When we have no need of dying we shall no longer die. This I believe!

Immortal Journey

I hope you don't think I'm going on eternally. I always remember a story Mark Twain used to tell.

He found himself in a little town and he didn't have anything else to do, so he went out to see what was going on. He came upon a revival meeting and went in. The evangelist was pleading with the people to give to the missions in Africa. He was a good speaker. After Twain had listened to him for ten minutes, he thought, "When they pass the plate around, I'm gonna put $50 in it." After he listened for thirty minutes, he decided to make it $10. After he listened for another hour, he thought, "I think I'll make it $5." An hour after that, Twain said, "When they finally passed the plate around, I stole $2 out of it.''

I'd like us to consider a little longer how we can expect to recognize in another life those who have been dear to us in this one, if we only believe in reincarnation. As I've told you, I hope to recognize my dear ones, as much as anyone does. I believe I will. How will I do it? I'll do it just as I did this time. How did I recognize my dear ones this time? Very simply. They were dear. That's all. They were dear.

We want to be with those we love as much as we can. We find we have much in common with them—common interests, and even more, common feelings and attitudes. We have the same yearnings—and mostly we yearn to be with one another. We need to draw close to those we love. We want to know as much about them as we can. We feel we are one with them. What happens to them happens to us. We rejoice in their joys, and sorrow in their sorrows. We triumph in their triumphs, and suffer with them in their defeats. We're drawn to those we love by deep and, mainly, I'm sure, unconscious longings.

My wife didn't come up to me with a little sign, W-I-F-E. If she had, I would probably have run in the other direction. Maybe she had the little sign hidden down underneath.

She was from southern Louisiana; I was born in Delaware; we met in Missouri; and we were attracted to one another. She was dear to me and I was dear to her. That's all. And so, we've liked being with one another, sharing life. She'll always be dear to me. I'll always be dear to her, I believe.

It's only blood relatives who come announced, and we've got—what?—a fifty-fifty chance of liking them? When we're little, somebody comes up to us and says, "Jimmy, this is your dear Aunt Minerva," and we let out a howl and run behind Mama's skirts. Aunt Minerva may not appeal to us at all. Some of us even howl at our mothers. I've known a few kids who've kicked mama hard. Parents and children don't necessarily find each other dear.

As I told you, I never felt close to my father. Actually, I hardly got to know him. But what little knowledge I had didn't endear him to me. Who knows? Maybe if I got to know him in an entirely different context, I might grow to understand him and even learn to like him and enjoy being with him. But the thought of the me I now am spending eternity with the him he was is a very unhappy one. We had no common interests or viewpoints and, I'm sorry to say, little love.

That's the way it is with many blood relatives. We recognize the people dear to us, not because they come announced but because we find ourselves drawn to them, and that is the sole and natural way. That is the way it's always going to be, in this life or any other. If you think about it, it's the only way it could be. I believe it's the only way you would want it.

Also, we sometimes recognize people who aren't dear to us, and we shrink back from them, and we'll always do that, too. I hope that, as we live other lives, we'll be growing spiritually and we'll understand other people better and be more loving and forgiving, so there'll be more and more people dear to us and fewer and fewer "un-dear." But we're going to be drawn to people and repelled by people, just as we were here, because we like to be with them or we don't like to be with them. We share thoughts and feelings and experiences with those we love, and we find joy in their company.

Think about how those who are dear to you became dear to you. Perhaps some who are dear to you have always been dear to you. You can't remember a time when they weren't. Some were dear to you instantly, the moment you met them. Some became dear to you slowly. Sometimes we don't like people when we first meet them, but after a while we become dearly attracted to them. Sometimes we like people, but after a while we don't. That's the way it's always going to be. How else could it be and make sense? Some who are dear to us will always be dear. Some who are not dear to us will always be not dear. Some who are dear to us will become unendeared. And some who are not dear to us will become dear.

One of the best friends I ever had I didn't like at all when we first knew each other. Then we became dear friends, and for years our lives were close. Then our lives separated. I haven't seen him for years and years. I don't know, maybe we'd be friends if we met again; maybe we wouldn't. We may have moved in entirely different directions. In other lives it will be like this too. Dear ones won't come announced. They'll be dear because they're dear—or they won't be.

As I say, some will grow slowly to be dear, some will attract us instantly. Haven't you met someone and instantly thought, "Oh, I want to know that man," or "I've got to know that woman"? Instantly. I've had that experience a number of times. I believe everyone has.

Not long ago I was on a lecture trip and a couple was appointed to take me to one town from another. I've had that happen when it wasn't a very happy experience. So I usually stay pretty much inside myself for a while. But I wasn't with this couple ten minutes before we became dear friends, and we still are. I long to be with them. If I'm anywhere within hundreds of miles, we get together. When my wife met them, she loved them too, just as quickly as I did. We count them among our dearest friends.

I've had such an experience a number of times; not too often, because we don't have that many people we're strongly drawn to.

But all of us have had the experience of walking into a room and finding ourselves irresistibly drawn to a certain person.

My mother told me when I was a little boy, they put me in a kindergarten that was located in a church in a Polish neighborhood. There was a little Polish boy there. I couldn't speak a word of Polish and he couldn't speak a word of English. My mother said we were a nuisance to the teacher because, no matter how she tried to separate us, in two minutes we'd be back together again, with our arms around one another. I don't have any idea who that little Polish boy was. He went his way in life and I've gone mine. But there must have been some deep attraction between us for us to act as we did, and for such an immediate and intense relation to spring up.

Reincarnation is an explanation for such an attraction. As Dr. Stevenson pointed out, when we're children, there is much more likelihood of memories of a former life staying with us. But I wonder if we might not have memories we can't express in words. Words are at the topmost layer of the pile when you think of what a human being is—spirit, mind, and body. They're the latest acquisition in the evolution of the human mind. It's reasonable to think they'd be the first element of mind we'd let go. But I wonder if we don't often remember, not in words, but in our fibers, in the deep unconscious layers of our being that were there before we learned to think in words. And so, without words, but with deep-felt longings for which we have no words, we are drawn.

I remember an experience I once had when I happened to attend a horse show. There was a family performing in the show. They traveled about performing in such shows. I believe they were Hungarian. The girls rode horseback, doing acrobatic feats. Beyond one end of the main arena, there was a large area where people mingled between events, buying drinks and snacks. There was a small roped-off area at the far side of this large room, where performers could be separated from the crowd. The room was jammed with hundreds of people. I went into the room, and across it, probably a hundred feet away, I saw that one of the girls had come out and was standing at the edge of her small roped-off area. Across that room, across all those people, the girl and I looked at one another. Immediately I felt that this strange girl and I knew one another. In fact, I felt a tremendous attraction surge between us. Suddenly the girl ducked under the rope and began to thread her way across that milling crowd. It was not an easy passage, for the milling crowd made a moving maze. It took her several minutes to make her way through it, but there was no doubt when our eyes met through the mass of people, she was coming to me.

I wish I had an interesting ending for this story, but I don't. I'm a coward. Because there were so many people in the room, from time to time the girl would be engulfed by them and disappear. At one of these times, I turned away and hurried back into the main arena where my wife was waiting for me in the grandstand. But there's never been any doubt in my mind, I knew that girl and she knew me, although I don't know how or when. But there was some kind of unfinished business between us. Because I'm a coward, a married coward, I left it for another life to find out what it is.

I remember another person I met that way. This one was a young man, so I was braver. Again we met in a room packed with people, and again we were immediately drawn. The moment we met we were close friends. Extraordinarily strong feelings ran between us. But almost immediately it was also apparent, these feelings were deeply ambivalent. We loved one another and hated one another. We lived in different cities, so we only saw one another occasionally. When we did, it was as if we were brothers—brothers who loved each other dearly, had always known each other. But every time we met, very shortly, it was also apparent that mixed with the love there was anger, which certainly in this life there was no accounting for.

I'm sure psychologists can find some sort of polysyllabled explanation for such experiences as these. But if you've ever had them, you know how intense they are, and how unexplainable. Haven't all of us had such experiences? When we meet people this way, there's always a tremendous sense that we know them and know them well.

For myself, I don't think there's any explanation as satisfactory as that we knew each other from a former life. As I've said about the people we love in this life, if somewhere we meet again, we'll recognize each other, and we'll recognize each other as we recognized each other in this life. We will be drawn, but it won't be superficially. It won't be by resemblances of face or recollection of past lives and old relationships. We'll be drawn deeply, by bonds of love and common purpose, by mutual attraction of mind and spirit, by a communion that's not of words or even thoughts, but an inward oneness. We'll be drawn by the same spontaneous springing up of recognition that drew us together here, brother with brother, mother with child, husband with wife, friend with friend. Heart will speak to heart, and that is a language all of us understand. That's the way it's always been; that's the way it always will be. That's the only way it could be.

I believe we will be reunited with those we love because always we'll be living at the level of consciousness we have attained. That's the only kind of life that's possible. Those we love will be drawn to us because they're at our level of consciousness, too.

But I don't think I'll look like what I look like now, and I don't think they'll look like whatever it was they looked like when they were part of my life. No, if we reunite, it will be the "I" I have come to be and the "you" you have come to be. Life is change and growth, and if we keep on living beyond this life, we're going to keep on growing, we're going to keep on changing, as we have in this life, and as we always will.

Several years ago a dear friend of mine died, and one day, shortly after her death, I was sitting looking out at the ocean and suddenly a piece of verse came into my mind. Let me read it:

All you I have loved who are no more,
My lovely ladies and gentlemen,
I love you still as I did before,
And I pray we may meet again,
Though I don't know how that may be or
        where,
In another time and another space,
What name or number we may bear,
Or even what form or face,
But whatever I have for a heart will leap,
And we will turn and know and touch,
For, O my lovelies, love runs deep,
And I have loved you much.

I believe that's the way it will be, and I want it to be that way. I certainly wouldn't want to think I've come as far as I can go, that I can be no more than what I now am. I've grown and changed in this life, and having grown, I can see how much more I can be than what I have become.

I don't want to stand still. I want to become yet more. I want to be the yet more I sense I'm capable of being, however far and to whatever undreamed-of experiences that may take me. Don't you? Would you like forever to be what you now are? Or even what you were at the absolute peak of your life?

If an angel came down to me at my happiest, most fulfilled moment, and said, "Hey, Jim, I can keep you right here, so that forever you will be just what you are now," I hope I'd be smarter than Faust was when Mephistopheles made him that same proposition. I hope I'd be wise enough and brave enough to say, "Get thee behind me, Angel." I don't want to stop, not even at the peak of happiness, though I don't think that's possible.

I am on an immortal journey, and I have yet more journeying to do.

Through chance and change, by way of worlds forgotten and courses unremembered yet graven in my soul, I came up to here, and from here, by ways unknown yet ways my soul has drawn me to, I journey on.

This is the human condition.

I have risen on innumerable mornings.

I have slept through innumerable nights.

I have journeyed on innumerable journeys.

I have lived in familiar and unfamiliar worlds.

I have had brave and beautiful companions, lovely friends. I shall have them yet again.

I have been weak and strong, wise and unwise.

I have come on much curious knowledge,

some remembered, some forgotten.

I have done many deeds, some worthy, some unworthy.

What I am undertaking I am not sure—but somehow I am sure it is an enterprise worthy of my effort.

Where I am going I am not sure—but I am sure it is a destination worthy of myself.

Here I am at this place on this day.

Tonight I shall lie down once more to sleep, and tomorrow I shall rise again and journey on.

I am glad that on this journey, dear friend, I have met in this place for these few pleasant hours to share my thoughts with you.

About the Author

James Dillet Freeman retired in 1984 from his position as a member of the board of trustees and first vice president of Unity School, and continues to speak and write for the worldwide Unity movement. He served the School for more than fifty years. For thirteen years, he served as director of Silent Unity. In 1983 he resigned the directorship in order to devote more time to writing and speaking. Jim is an ordained Unity minister and former director of Unity's ministerial training program.

In speaking to the question: What does it mean to be a minister? he says, "It means to be God-centered and human-hearted; to involve yourself in man's humanity and to keep your vision on man's divinity."

Born in Wilmington, Delaware, Jim moved to Kansas City with his family when he was ten years old. He attended Kansas City public schools and the University of Missouri, where he was graduated with honors in 1932. He began writing verse at the age of ten, and by the time he finished college, his poems had been published in national publications.

While still in college, he was given summer work at Unity School by invitation of Unity's cofounder, Myrtle Fillmore. After a year of postgraduate work at the University, he joined the Unity staff on a permanent basis, serving the School's prayer ministry as a letter writer.

As a poet and author, Jim has inspired millions. He is a modern-day transcendentalist, in the tradition of Emerson, Thoreau, and Whitman. The universal appeal of his work has prompted translations in thirteen languages. His work has been published in The New Yorker, Saturday Review, Scientific Monthly, Christian Herald, Good Housekeeping, McCall's, The New York Times, and Reader's Digest, among others. Jim has also written twelve books.

Jim's widest acclaim has come from his poetry. It is estimated that published copies of his poems exceed 300 million. His work has been taken to the moon twice, a distinction he shares with no other author. His "Prayer for Protection," written in 1941, was taken to the moon on Apollo XI in July 1969 by Lunar Module pilot Edwin E. Aldrin, Jr. Aldrin had the poem with him when he made his historic moonwalk. Two years later, "I Am There," a poem written in 1947, went to the moon with Colonel James B. Irwin on the Apollo XV flight. Irwin left a microfilm copy of the poem on the moon.

Jim Freeman has the unique ability to speak as well as he writes. Lecture tours have taken him across the United States many times, and to Canada, Europe, and the West Indies. He has appeared as a guest on radio and television programs throughout North America.

Jim is married. He and his wife, Billie, make their home in Lee's Summit, Missouri. An ordained Unity minister, Mrs. Freeman is a former Unity School employee. She served for more than fifty years in Silent Unity as a writer, teacher, editor, and administrator.

Printed U.S.A.

179-F-8914-10M-9-86